The 7 Mind-Sets for a Fit Life

Developing the Mental Muscles for Success, Health and Happiness

Christine,
To your massive
transformation into
happiness, health & fulfillment.
Much love,
Alex 4/11/20

ALEX GIL

Table of Contents

Preface

For a very long time, I have been wanting to write a book about human potential. How do we really live our highest potential in this life? If we just have one lifetime and one chance, how can we make it the very best?

About five years ago, when I was going through some life transitions, I became extremely curious about my own potential. I started evaluating myself deeply, like my thoughts, my behaviors, and my patterns. It was a time that I fully embodied the concept that we are true creators, and we are responsible for all our actions and the results we get in life. We participate in everything, we are never passive victims. So I started a journey of study, research, and deep curiosity about how we change, how we create something out of nothing, how people go from broke to rich, sick to healthy, miserable to happy—basically how we transform our lives.

I am about to share concepts with you that are not new; in fact, for many of you it might be common sense. If you say it is all common sense, though, then the question becomes, are you applying the concepts in your own life? Knowledge is not power unless it is applied. I assure you, I have applied everything in this book to my own life. I wanted this book to be authentic, based on methods that I know work because they have worked for me and my clients. While I have added my own insights to established methods, they are all based on Universal Laws, a common language that you will find in other literature.

So what is different about this book? First, let me ask you a couple questions: How do you live your highest potential every day in your life? If we just have one shot, how can you do the very best and have no regrets? Some of you may say we have many lives, if you believe in reincarnation (and I do believe in that, too). But let's keep it simple here and talk about the life we have now—our conscious reality—because, after all, today is all we have control of, truly.

"You are today where your thoughts have brought you;
you will be tomorrow where your thoughts take you."

— *JAMES ALLEN*

Based on the writings of James Allen and many other incredible philosophers from the late 19th and early 20th centuries, we are masters of our thoughts, and our thoughts become our reality. That is one of the most important discoveries we have made as humans. This means that we have an incredible power to manage our lives, our outcomes, and our results.

This book is more than a book about managing your thoughts; it is a book about managing yourself, about being a leader of your life to create health, happiness, and success, because you are wired to be healthy and happy. It is your nature.

"The greatest revolution of my generation is the
discovery that people, by changing their inner attitudes
of mind, can change the outer aspects of their lives."

— *WILLIAM JAMES*

As a human potential and performance coach, I see clients every day who are at a point in their lives where they know changes need to be made. They want to improve their quality of life and sense of well-being. They know they can do better and they *want* to do better. They seek strategies and solutions on how to feel happier, how to have more energy, how to find more balance and peace of mind.

I have so much faith in every single one of my clients that they can create the life they want. We all can. If I did it, you can do it. If Oprah Winfrey did it, you can do it, too. If Tony Robbins and many other role models and leaders out there can transform their lives, so can you. It is so easy to separate ourselves from extraordinary people. I did that for most of my life until a few years ago, when I started studying the mind and read the stories of many successful people. I discovered that they were all ordinary people, just like you and me. They had struggles, tough childhoods, experienced poverty or abuse. They overcame their traumas, the struggles, and the challenges that left scars in their souls. They did not let the pain define who they were. They gathered their strength, resilience, and toughness that developed over the years and used those qualities to transform themselves, and with that they created extraordinary lives. I was intrigued and, at the same time, inspired by so many stories. I became curious and my journey exploring human potential took off. I want to share with you what I have discovered so far.

After coaching clients for more than 20 years, mostly as a personal trainer, I have watched many people do everything "right" and still not achieve the results they wanted. This is the very reason why five years ago I decided to shift my career path into holistic lifestyle coaching. As a trainer, I focused on exercise, nutrition, and overall wellness. I would design my clients' diet and training programs, and if they followed it, they should lose weight and get healthier, right? Well, I came to find out, this was not necessarily true. There were many pieces missing, which led me on a path of research.

I became a ferocious reader and student of health, happiness, stress, and the *mind*. I was determined to learn why some people succeed and others don't. Initially I made assumptions that the ones who don't succeed just lack discipline, they are lazy, they don't want something bad enough, or they settle for mediocrity. But the issue is more complicated than that. I say complicated because many of these issues that are holding people back from living their best life exist underneath the obvious behaviors. They live under the veil, so to speak. **These are our deep-seated beliefs of how we truly see ourselves and what we think is possible for ourselves.**

This book is a guide for you to start creating the success you want. It is a guide that will teach you what MIND-SETS you need to develop in order to face the challenges you will have along the way—and you will have challenges. However, with the right mind-set, the proper attitude, and inner strength you can get through anything without losing yourself in the process and without sacrificing your health and happiness. There is no doubt that getting what we want in life does involve sacrifices. But people are confused about what sacrifices really are. Most people have the belief that you must sacrifice your well-being in order to create success. That is not success. My definition of success is to have a life that is filled with vibrant health and high levels of energy, surrounded by love, happiness, and financial abundance. Financial abundance without life force, love, and happiness is not success in my dictionary.

This book is not about a magic formula of success. This book is about coaching you in how to do the work yourself and create the life you deserve, an extraordinary life. I am not going to give you the fish, I am going to teach you how to fish. You must do the work, but I can guarantee this: you will grow by doing the work I propose in this book, you will get to know yourself deeper, and, with daily practice and mastery, you will succeed.

One of the things I am going to teach you is how to find the beliefs that are blocking your way to success. Then I will help you understand them, learn how to take their force away, and learn how to replace them with beliefs that will juice your life, your energy, and your dreams. In other words, you will train your brain to think in a way that aligns with the outcome you want.

I want to share with you all the tools I know and have applied in my own life that have created great success, a consistent state of joy, and high levels of energy. These tools are not new, they were not invented by me or one specific person. They are based on the laws of life; they are Universal principles of energy that we put into thoughts, actions, and feelings. I will coach you in how to amplify your energy and direct it—this is self-management mastery that you can obtain with practice and discipline. It takes energy to change.

Brendon Burchard, performance coach and author of *The Charge*, always says that we are like a power plant—we don't have energy, we generate energy. I will add that we have the most incredible power to influence the energy that we create, we have the superpower of directing that energy toward anything and anyone. We have the superpower to manifest anything we want, even the impossible. Look at the car you are driving, airplanes, rockets, your smartphone—all the machines that once were thought to be impossible. But at some point, someone had an idea, a concept, and the *belief* that the impossible was actually possible. They were called crazy, they were judged, criticized, and failed many times, but they kept going because they had *grit*. What was their secret? Obsession, you say? Some of that, sure. But before that, they also had a vision, and they became present with that vision and held onto it every single day. They worked obsessively on that vision and had the MIND-SET that "anything is possible and what I don't know I will learn as I go."

I want YOU to be that MIND-SET. You have the same superpowers as Thomas Edison, Steve Jobs, Steven Spielberg, Oprah Winfrey, Benazir Bhutto, Amelia Earhart, and many others. The difference is that they did not let their limiting beliefs stop them. They were not paralyzed by their fear, but rather they focused on what they wanted to create and they moved through the fear and challenges to reach success.

This conversation is so important to me because it has the power to set you free and to empower you, so you can be your super you. Let's do a quick test here: how many times have you looked at someone because of who they are or what they created and said to yourself, I could never do that, I don't have the skills, the intelligence, the money, the education. This is the source of living a small life. The "I am not good enough" syndrome that drives millions of people to the therapist's office. This syndrome creates depression, anxiety, and many other illnesses because a physical illness is mostly a reflection of an illness in the mind and soul. I see many who spent years in the therapist's office and they are still living a much smaller life than they want and deserve. Why? It's simple: they talked, talked, talked but never changed their deep-seated beliefs, they never changed their mind-set, and they never explored their unconscious beliefs that were driving their thoughts, behaviors, and attitudes. That is why we are having this conversation.

Authentic changes don't need to take years, months, or even weeks, it can happen now. It will take vulnerability, courage, focus, confidence, and hard work at times. I will teach you step-by-step how to do this work, where to put your focus, what questions you must answer for yourself, and provide an action plan to serve as your road map. You are my client now; I will share with you the same framework I teach my private clients and the same tenets that I use to teach a seven-hour class at my studio in Boulder, Colorado. I want this teaching to impact everyone, to inspire you to do your inner work because I want you to be happy, healthy, and have tremendous success in your life.

‍

A Little Bit About Me

I have not always been thriving to be my best, to be extraordinary. I don't think I even used the word "extraordinary" growing up. I am a native of Brazil and lived in the suburbs of São Paulo until I was 26 years old. It was interesting living there; I felt like an outsider my whole life, even though I was born there. I am an only child and have a typical story of my parents getting divorced when I was 10. I was confused, lonely, and lost.

Thankfully, I had two strong women in my life: my mother and my grandmother. They provided different needs. My mother was the financial provider, she made sure we had plenty of food, all the toys I wanted, and a nice place to live. She was not very nurturing or very expressive, however she was a hard worker, honest, and full of integrity. She had a kind soul and always helped family members in need.

My grandmother was my rock, my love, my caretaker. In the Brazilian culture, it is very common for kids to be taken care of by their grandmothers. The parents work, and the grandmother comes to live with the family. It is a gift in my culture because they love their grandkids like their own. My grandmother had her issues; she was bitter, with reason. Her husband had just walked out one day and never came back, and she was left with six children to care for. That left scars. We loved each other so much but we fought a lot. We both were not getting our needs met. I wanted the love of my mother, wanted her to be home, wanted her attention. Grandmother wanted a different life. It was a loving yet volatile relationship. However, she taught me unconditional love.

In 1994 I graduated from college and got a job as a personal trainer. Personal training was just coming to Brazil; we were always behind the trends in the United States. I started to become more independent, made some money, dated, played, and traveled a bit. Still, something inside me never felt right. I was not fit for the lifestyle in Brazil—drinking, partying, marrying young, kids. I felt lonely, I felt disconnected. I was craving adventure. I had a call to explore and I always knew the United States was my calling. So in 1996, I heard it loud and clear. I figured out a way to save $2,000 to go to California and take a ten-week English class at the University of California San Diego. I had a catalyst, though—a feisty and courageous friend named Karen. She was well traveled, a fireball. She inspired me. She went to California first, and three months later I followed her.

I will never forget the day I landed in San Diego. I felt like I was in a playground. Imagine a girl who had always lived in the ugly suburbs of São Paulo (one of the biggest cities in the world) seeing people rollerblading all over the boardwalk, playing beach volleyball, coffee shops everywhere—this was not a concept in Brazil at that time. People were vibrant and happy. There were beautiful bodies and people everywhere I looked. I was in a fantasy land! I met so many cool international students, was exposed to fun parties at the beach, I watched sunsets every day. I was happy, I was finding myself. With only $2000 in my pocket that did not last long and speaking no English at all, somehow I made a life in the United States work. I made my dream come true. I knew this dream was possible and it became my reality. This journey has been beautiful, bumpy, hard at times, but incredibly rich. I have created a life in Boulder, Colorado, that is the most fulfilling life I could hope for. My work is my calling and my passion. My family is made of my friends, my partner, my dog, and my cat. I am surrounded by nature and an incredible community. This is home.

_____

About This Book

If you are reading this book it is because you are looking for better or different ways to make authentic changes in your life. Or you want to try different strategies because the ones you have tried before may not be working anymore. You may be looking for ways to take your personal growth to the next level and to understand how you can utilize the power of your mind to support you and develop a deeper relationship with the self. Whatever your journey is, I am here for you. It is my deep desire that this book will offer you insights that will help you have higher levels of energy, cultivate happiness, and create vibrant health. Through your choices, you will be a success. My definition of success is a life that is lived with purpose, passion, and a deep sense of fulfillment. Fulfillment that comes with abundant love, health, spirituality, service, connections, and financial abundance.

We can have it all. I want you to get this concept right way as you embark on this journey with me. I am not saying that you won't make sacrifices, but as I mentioned before, you will not sacrifice your peace, health, or well-being. You may sacrifice time with friends, that three-hour bike ride, or a vacation, but it will be easy to sacrifice those things temporarily because you will be engaged working on your dream. It is not hard to say no to a beach vacation when you are focused and happy being productive, and you are creating a life that can give you many beach vacations in the future.

Many say the secret to success is hard work. This is true, but we need to be clear that we want to work hard on a path that has meaning to us.

The stress that comes from doing what we love does not kill us, it makes us stronger, happier, and more resilient.

My request: Open your mind, let go of attachments to your old beliefs or ways of doing things. Be courageous and honest with yourself, be vulnerable, and be curious. Be a student of life, learn, reflect, and, most importantly, apply the knowledge you learn here.

Read this book with a highlighter and mark anything that speaks to you. Have a pen handy and make side notes. Have a small journal with you as you read to jot down personal insights because I will trigger your creativity, I will challenge you at times, and I will invite you to reflect. At the end of each chapter, I will ask you to answer a few questions that will help you embody the chapter material, like an exercise to work the mind muscle. These sessions will be called "Journal Time." Each chapter contains specific questions that will help you unlock beliefs, feelings, and emotions. Read this book in sequence and do the exercises in sequence. This is important because at the end of the book, you will have your blueprint for happiness, health, and success. It will be your road map, your guide with affirmative thoughts that align with your life vision and actions that are congruent with your desires. And the best part is that new beliefs will be formed that will work for you and for your dreams—no more beliefs that work against you.

I am super excited to have you here with me, I am honored to be your teacher, and I am fulfilled to be of service for our humanity and our planet. A person who is happy, healthy, and fulfilled will not hurt another, will not mistreat an animal, will not destroy our beautiful planet Earth—that is why I am writing this book.

Let's go together and make this place better than we found it. Let's make our journey through this life extraordinary. Let me help you so you can become the best version of yourself.

Peace and love,
Alex

Introduction

My first contact with the teachings about the power of the mind came in 1999 when one of my clients gave me a copy of Brian Tracy's book *Maximum Achievement*. He talks about the power of affirmation, a strategy that works to program our subconscious mind to work for us. I was not even 30 years old yet. I read the book and put it to the side. That was the beginning of a lot of reading for me; I was fascinated about human potential. Many of those books are in the category of self-help. Self-help does not resonate with me as much as human potential or personal growth and personal development do. I want to call this book category "personal development": a book to help you grow into the person you are meant to be, the person you are designed to be. This is a guide that will help you close that gap between the person you are now and the person you want to be, your ideal self. There should not be any gap, but there is, with all of us. Closing that gap is a daily spiritual work, a work of *awareness* during those moments of incongruence. We must notice those moments so we can bring ourselves right back to congruence and to balance. That is how we create peace of mind. Our bodies are constantly telling us, "This feels right" or "This does not feel right."

Awareness is a prerequisite to growth and change. The word "change" bothers me sometimes even though I know we all change. I have changed tremendously in the last 10 years or so. But what if we don't change? What if we simply let go of the parts of ourselves that are not serving us, the masks and personas that we use daily to survive, to "fit in"? By letting go of these parts, we start to get in touch with who we truly are, or what is called our authentic self. We start seeing our true essence, and in that process we open our hearts fully to love and be loved. It is a game changer.

We don't change, we transform. I believe that we don't change because we are born perfect, we are born with a soul imprint of our personality and our life's purpose. We don't change. **Our thoughts, patterns, and behaviors change, therefore, we transform.** We are simply in the journey of getting to our true selves, that is our spiritual work. The most important work we can do daily is our inner work—to develop such a deep knowledge of who we are, what we love, and what our purpose is. What is our life's mission, our essential needs, our core values in all areas of our lives? These aspects are the foundation of our life and they give us daily guidance for our actions, thoughts, and behaviors. So, if we don't have all these aspects clear in our **conscious mind,** our control center, then who is running our show? Who is determining our actions, thoughts, and behaviors? A default system called the **subconscious mind** is. Do you have behaviors or patterns that you feel just happen and that you have a sense you have no control over them? Or are there times when you say, "I don't know what came over me or what made me to do that"? We all experience these moments. What is driving our behaviors is our subconscious mind, the real commander.

This book will explore the mind-sets that are necessary to make you emotionally and mentally fit. Think of these mind-sets as mental muscles that you need to develop to be fit for life.

I will give you strategies that you can apply to your daily life that will give you great results. Therefore, I will keep all the scientific information to a very small part of your reading. I am coaching you, and as your coach, I will give you sound and applicable solutions.

Science of the Mind and Beliefs

To define the mind, I am going to use the words of Dr. Daniel Siegel: "The mind is an embodied process that regulates the flow of energy and information." What he means by that is our mind is a complex system that is constantly taking information from external sources like our environment, people, and situations and then translating it into energy that feeds our emotions. Before it feeds our emotions—this is very important to note—that energy feeds a belief that lives in our minds. A belief is a thought that we have over and over; it is what forms our life choices and systems. Based on the power of that belief or thought, we will have an emotional response to the environment, people, and situations. So here is the greatest gift and power within: if we want to change how we feel, how we respond or react—our actions and our results— then we must go to the source of it all. Our deep-seated beliefs and our daily thoughts that are empowering and feeding those beliefs are the source.

I will be sharing a step-by-step map of how you can identify those beliefs and how to know if they serve you or if they don't. You will learn how to change them and how to reprogram your beliefs system in order to change the results in your life.

Think about the last time you tried to lose weight, make more money, or change a relationship dynamic and gave up because you got tired of trying. Did you try making those changes by relying on external resources? External resources are usually distractions that we rely on expecting them to bring change, like trying to find a shortcut to avoid the deeper work of shifting and/or creating new mind-sets. Examples of external resources are reading self-help books and not applying what you learn or going to therapy and doing all the talking without making internal changes. It could also be following a diet and exercise plan without believing that you deserve to lose the weight. Most likely it worked a little but did not create the results you wanted. Earlier I mentioned that many times we do "everything" right and don't get the outcome we want. Why? Because we are trying too hard in the wrong place.

Think about lifting a heavy object using two long pieces of two-by-four wood, like a lever. What happens if you place them at the wrong angle and apply force at the wrong section? You can barely move that object. Slide the wood deeper underneath the object, move your hands farther down, and with less effort you are able to move the object. Similarly, you aren't doing the wrong thing by trying hard or relying on your willpower to create changes in your life. It is just not as efficient that way, and it takes enormous amounts of energy and time, plus creates frustration, which leads to an "I give up" attitude when you are almost there.

So, I am saying that you are almost there already. I know that because you are reading this book. All you need now is a tweak, to adjust your angle of holding the wood a little. Don't underestimate the power in the "little angle." Just think what would happen if a cruise ship from the United States heading to Japan changed its angle a little. It changes the destination completely over a period of time. Less is more! I will be referring to this philosophy a lot throughout the book, so you may as well highlight it now.

The Seven Mind-Sets

1. Awareness

If **awareness** is the prerequisite for growth, we need to understand fully what it means to be aware. How can we be attentive to our thoughts without taking away the joy of the present and without feeling we are "working" all the time? In chapter 1, I will present to you easy ways to be aware without a lot of effort, to be an observer without judgment, to be able to shift your focus in a second and change your perception, and, therefore, enrich your experiences with people, situations, and life.

2. Beliefs

For deep assessments of our behaviors, patterns, thoughts, and emotions, we need to go to the root of it all: our **beliefs.** A belief is a thought that we have over and over; it gains energy, it gets dense, and it becomes a director of everything we do and think. For example, if you believe meat is bad for you, you won't eat it and it may make you have negative feelings toward those who are meat lovers, all because of that belief. In chapter 2, I will guide you step-by-step in defining and understanding how our beliefs system is fundamental to creating authentic changes and different outcomes in life.

3. CONFIDENCE

Speaking of beliefs, can you say you have **confidence** to create the life you want? Confidence that you can learn whatever you need to learn in order to succeed? Assuming you are a human like myself, your answer is probably, yes, in some areas and not at all in others. How do we bring confidence in areas that are crucial for our growth and success? You will learn how by understanding what kills confidence and what builds it. Confidence is like a muscle, you start the work before you see the muscle developing and put the time to build that strength, it does not happen overnight but it takes less time that you think. In chapter 3, I will teach you how to build the confidence muscle, core mental muscle that will help you face fear to move through tough times.

4. DRIVE

In the process of building our confidence muscle, we need to find what **drives** us. What is the fuel and the motive that makes us get up in the morning and do the work, that pushes us to show up at our best? Drive gets us moving toward actions with purpose. With drive we want to learn new skills, study, go to seminars, and work out every day. Drive is generated from our big dreams. The core elements of drive are desire, momentum, attitude, and energy. I will be discussing each one of those elements in chapter 4.

5. EMOTIONAL FITNESS

Even when we have great tools for success and plan things with caution, we still face setbacks and disappointments. We lose, we fail, we freeze, and we question our capacity to handle the stress that comes with the pursuit of anything that matters to us. The fundamental mind-set muscle for life's challenges is emotional intelligence, which I call in this book **emotional fitness.** The ability to control and manage our emotions is absolutely fundamental to be successful in any area of our lives. Our lives are about connections and relationships. Being fit emotionally helps us to master communication, an essential skill for successful living. In chapter 5, I will teach you what the most important aspects of emotional fitness are and how to exercise each one.

6. Fearlessness

What if you have many of these traits already and still feel blocked or stuck at times? Maybe you need to get very cozy with fear. You need to learn how to have **fearlessness** so you can cultivate courage. In chapter 6, I will teach you how to face fear head on, how to disarm it, and how to develop deeper levels of courage, a must-have muscle to live your full potential. You will learn how to make friends with fear and use it to your advantage.

So what if you have tried "everything" for a long time and still have not achieved the results you want? You have awareness, belief in yourself, confidence, a drive to succeed, a fearless attitude, and you are fit emotionally, yet you've missed the deadline you gave to yourself. You've hit a big bump in the road and you start questioning your skill set. What is missing and what else can you develop to help you?

7. Grit

There is another quality that you must acquire as a warrior of life: **grit**. Grit is not about working really hard toward something, and it's not about intensity. Grit is about sustainable belief, sustainable energy, and sustainable focus. In chapter 7 I will be sharing what fuels grit and how you can master this mind-set that is essential for a badass successful life, because that is what you are designed to create.

So the first thing I ask you to do before we move forward together is to say the following sentence out loud, and then write it down in the space below.

"I am absolutely capable of creating the life I want and deserve. I am ready, I am ready, I AM READY. I am ready to live my fullest potential."

Now, your turn.

_____

_____

_____

_____

By: _____

One

*I know who I am, I know my deepest fears, I
know my dreams, I know the voices of my ego and
the echo of my shadows. I know the reflections of
my light and the frequency of my heart. I know
when my heart speaks and my ego screams.*

Before we dive into what awareness is and how to master it, I need to
walk you through the different layers of the mind. What is the mind,
again? As defined by Dr. Daniel Siegel (and as I shared in the introduc-
tion), "The mind is an embodied process that regulates the flow of energy
and information."

Think of the mind as our antenna. It grabs what is around us—energy
and information—and translates it into thoughts, feelings, and emotions.
Imagine you are sitting with a group of people you don't know well and
someone says something that you strongly disagree with. At the second
you hear the statement that you dislike, a reaction occurs in your body,
and you feel constriction, maybe anger, and a strong desire to express your
charged emotions and thoughts. That is your mind. The conscious and
the subconscious parts of you went into alert, and you picked up information that did not resonate with your belief system. Maybe even energy

1

prior to that existed because you did not feel a connection with that person, for no particular reason. Flow of energy and information flood our minds constantly, and every single thought, response, reaction, and emotion regarding that energy and information gets generated from our deep beliefs. If you follow this thought process, it is easy to understand why, when wanting to change our life's outcome, circumstances, and experiences, there is only one place to head first: **our belief system, the creator of all our experiences.**

"The unaware life is not worth living."

— SOCRATES

Awareness is a prerequisite to transformation and growth. We must understand our feelings, emotions, and actions in order to transform them. We must know the root of the behavior. This process of understanding is done with gentleness, compassion, and acceptance; it isn't done by criticism and judgment. We all got here to this present day carrying past experiences, sometimes traumas and hardship, from childhood or earlier adulthood. These experiences left a mark inside us, a mark that can manifest in the form of anger, resentment, mistrust, pain, and other negative emotions. I only call them negative because they don't serve us when held for a long period of time. Actually carrying these negative emotions inside takes energy, our life force. Pain needs energy to survive, energy that can be used as a fuel to support you in your dreams and goals. Don't keep carrying pain in your heart. It is okay, more than okay, to get angry at times, to feel hurt, to feel pain, and to shout because someone pissed you off. What is not okay is to give energy and focus to those emotions and make a story in your mind that will become a new belief.

Throughout this book I will be writing a lot about our stories, how we are the masters in creating stories in our heads, and how the stories become the chief of our actions, thoughts, and behaviors. Do you ever say to yourself something like, "It's not my fault I feel this way, it is my dysfunctional mother that made me this way"? Let's get clear about something right away. **In order to be a mature, healthy adult and lead a spiritual path, you must commit to stopping the blame game right now.** If you are reading this book, you are an adult, you are old enough to understand that **you are responsible for your thoughts, actions, and behaviors.** No one makes you do or feel anything that you don't want to. You may get hurt, sad, mad, but you should not sustain those emotions if you want to be free and happy. The choice to feed those emotions is entirely yours. The key is you experience them and let them go, because from this moment on, you choose to live in a state of joy, love, and abundance. These states cannot share space with negative emotions, so you must choose.

Now that you have chosen joy, love, and abundance you are open to learn new ways to tap into your superpowers, to become the extraordinary person that you are destined to be. **You are extraordinary, so don't choose an ordinary life.**

What other forces can dictate your actions? Let's take a look in the two main layers of our mind.

The Conscious And Subconscious Mind

Change your thoughts and your life changes.

Right now you could be thinking: I am hungry, I am cold, I need to pay my bills, I don't like someone's attitude, and so on. That is your conscious mind talking, it is your intellectual mind, making decisions all day long. It talks a lot. It is your commander mind and takes up about 5 percent of your mind function.

Now let's say, for example, you are reading this book in a café after having breakfast. Several things can be happening that you are not conscious of: your digestive system is breaking down sugars into glucose to feed your body's systems, you are breathing, and you are having an intuition about a person sitting next to you. That is all done by your subconscious mind.

It controls your bodily functions, it holds your short-term memory, it is intuitive, and it is your default mind.

Think of a time when you were driving and were having a great conversation with the passenger; you arrived at your destination and couldn't remember the way you drove. That is your default mind. Your subconscious mind took over your drive. The subconscious mind never stops working. It is the creator, the manifester, the one that really runs the show even though the conscious mind has the title of commander. The conscious mind has this title because it is the mind that programs our subconscious mind, so the subconscious mind obeys the commander.

Imagine you have told yourself over and over that dogs are vicious because you got bitten by a dog when you were four years old. Every time a dog approaches you, you have a physical reaction, a contraction in the chest and belly. Did you tell your body to contract? No, your subconscious did. **The greatest power within us is to redirect our attention, awareness, and focus to change the physical reaction and emotions of fear forever**. Let's imagine you make a decision to never fear dogs again. You find a nice dog and spend time petting and playing with that dog. You repeat this action over and over and ta-da!—no more fear or reactions when you see a dog. Nothing changed but your perception and belief. Everything else works the same way.

Our subconscious mind gets programmed by the conscious mind. These program codes run 24/7. Our subconscious mind delivers our feelings and emotions based on our old and new stories. Whatever we continuously think about will become the roots of those feelings and emotions. **This is why mastering your awareness is a must.** Become aware of when your body contracts, when you get moody, when you feel fearful, excited, happy, and relaxed.

Knowing ourselves well and exploring our feelings and emotions is necessary work to create a successful life. I see people become experts in computers, cars, politics, or any other science or subject and still lack the most important expertise: knowing their own mind and body. People eat foods that are basically dead foods and poisonous; they overeat, don't sleep enough; and they become overweight, sick, depressed, disconnected—all because they are asleep, they are in a state of complete unawareness. They are living in autopilot mode. Years go by and then, all of a sudden, some may ask, how did I get here? It's just like driving with your default system. This is why sometimes people who get cancer or have a heart attack change their lives completely. They wake up, they decide to become aware of their health, energy, and happiness. **Imagine if you direct your thoughts, energy, and focus into creating the exact life you want?** What would happen? How much more potential could you unleash? You would create unbelievable results—ideas, business, money that you never thought was possible. You can do it! You can do it by having full levels of awareness, deep focus, and taking relentless actions toward your dreams. Every thought, every action, every behavior will create an outcome, no matter what. It is the law of cause and effect. You may as well create the best outcome, don't you think? They all will take energy, so my goal for you is that you learn through this book how to direct all your energy into creating an extraordinary life.

Amplify Awareness

Let's get into how we develop high levels of awareness. Think of any quality in you that you want to focus on and strengthen, and begin to understand that it works like a muscle. You have an exercise, a practice, and you repeat it over and over. This is how we take any concept or idea and move from the intellectual mind into making every part of us believe and live that concept. We become *it*. Knowledge is not power unless it is applied and executed in your life every day. This is a process that I call embodiment. As new information is translated into a new habit that serves you, it moves from your conscious mind into your subconscious mind; it becomes part of you.

Awareness is the act of recognizing and understanding a feeling, a sensation, or an emotion. It speaks in the language of energy. That energy can be expressed physically, emotionally, mentally, and spiritually. It can be a feeling that something is wrong or about to happen, simply a tightness in your chest when you see someone from your past who hurt you, or an intuition about a decision you are about to make. It is a gut feeling then, you say? It can be. I call it more your intuition, which is an extension of awareness, a deep connection with your spirit. We can become so in tune with our bodies and our energy, and with that our intuitive intelligence gets stronger.

Your body is a full-time guide that is constantly telling you to go, stop, or slow down and think first. Use your senses to evaluate situations, which will lead to a shift in your thinking to therefore make a more just decision or choice.

For instance, you are going to a party and you are excited about it. However, the moment you walk in to this fun party, you sense your mood changing and feel a tightness in your throat and stomach. At that moment, can you stop and feel what is really happening? Can you be open and honest with yourself and point to what caused that contraction in your body, which will change your behavior and experience at the party? All of the sudden you won't have fun anymore, unless you address what is going on, change your perception, and make a decision to have fun no matter what. Unless, of course, you sense it is a dangerous place to be—that is when fear is healthy and you should run for your life. But in most cases, the fear that rises in the form of body contractions has nothing to do with a real danger, even though your body may be sending signals to your brain that you are in a state of fight or flight, and cortisol, a stress hormone, will be released into your bloodstream to help you "run." What is that fear? Is anyone at the party triggering your insecurity? Did anyone there cause you harm? Do you have an unresolved issue with someone? Are you feeling small in that crowd? Ask and you will find an answer. This is how you awaken your awareness muscle.

This is not hard work, but it does involve discipline and a deep sense of curiosity about yourself and your experiences. Don't make it too hard; simply notice feelings, body sensations, and thoughts as they come. Your body is talking to you all the time. You can feel when your body is relaxed, in bliss, or you can feel when your body is tight and stressed. The more you understand what is causing these experiences in your body and mind, the more aware you are. The more aware you are, the more in control you are of your thoughts, actions, and behaviors. Therefore, the more power you have to shift instantly. **Remember, we can't change what we can't understand. You can't heal what you can't feel.**

Once you master the skill of awareness, you are constantly shifting your mind, changing your attitude toward actions that better serve you, your vision, and others. I want to be clear, though, that when I use the word "master," I don't mean you know it all. Mastery is when you take a concept and fully embody it, live it, and practice it daily. It becomes part of your subconscious mind, part of your life-mastery skills. You understand it completely. That is mastery to me, and mastery gets better, sharper throughout our whole life. It does not plateau, which is a beautiful thing to know that we are always improving.

Pay attention, without judgment, without attachments. This is how your awareness will serve you best. Take what you see, take it all in as data, and process it, without qualifying the information into dualities like good or bad, right or wrong. Be an extraordinary observer of your internal experiences. You will learn so much about yourself; the more you practice awareness the deeper relationship you will have with yourself.

Inner Work

If you are physically fit, you probably spend time in the gym a few times a week lifting weights and either run, bike, or play a sport consistently. To be fit you also work on your nutrition, get good sleep, and take great care of your body. But what about being spiritually and emotionally fit? **What does it take to be a holistically fit human being?** Practice the strategies I share throughout this book and you will be a super-fit human being in every area.

To develop more awareness, I have designed a few exercises that will help you strengthen your awareness muscle.

Exercise #1: Breathe

This is one the most fundamental exercises for you to learn prior to meditation, strength training, yoga, and other forms of exercise to improve well-being. Most of us are not utilizing the power of our own breath. We have power to generate energy and change our physiology anytime we want, and it starts with the breath. We maintain our physiology in harmony by nourishing all the systems of our bodies. Remember biology class? Think about how each system of our body consists of millions of living organisms called cells. If some of these cells starve from oxygen because of shallow breathing or not enough breathing, you are depriving your body of major nourishment that creates energy.

Jack Angelo, in his book *Self-Healing with Breathwork,* states:

> *Full-breath breathing allows your abdomen, as well your chest, to fully expand as you inhale and to contract inward as you exhale. All the muscles of respiration are involved. This way of breathing opens your awareness to your moment-by-moment unity with the Source[1] and reeducates your physical body about efficient energy breathing, and thus maximizes your ability to take in available energies and to expel what is no longer required. Full-breath breathing rebalances the whole system, realigns all aspects of your being, and encourages the flow of healing energies.*

In other words, breathing deeply helps our nervous system to calm down. It is the greatest natural "chill pill." When you inhale deeply and expand your abdomen by sending 70 percent of your breath into the belly first and 30 percent into the chest, you are feeding every major system in the body: endocrine, respiratory, cardiovascular, muscular, and nervous.

---

1 Source can be defined as God, Spirit, Force, Universe, Soul, Energy, Buddha, Krishna, Christ, or any other being form that you connect with because of your religion or belief. I will use the term "Force" throughout the book.

When you take three to five minutes to practice what I call belly breathing, you are bringing yourself to the present moment, you are choosing to be aware of what is happening at that moment with your body. You are tapping into your inner intelligence, the one that comes from a place of deep wisdom, truth, and centered heart. Think of the times that you wish you had stopped to breathe before saying a hurtful word to someone you love. We have all done that, because those words come from a place of fear, a state of fight or flight, called the sympathetic system. When you stop and breathe deeply, you are turning on your relaxation system, called the parasympathetic system. This system has tremendous power to decrease the physiological effects of stress in our bodies. It allows us to handle situations of daily stress with ease, strength, and wisdom. Acting in this way you are what I call a stress warrior. It makes us aware of what is really going on, not just what our own perception is, which can many times mislead us to judgment and a reality that is not true. Breath is essential to the work of deep awareness.

"In the present moment, there is no stress."

— UNKNOWN

EXERCISE #2: OBSERVE

In conversations or disagreements, many times we talk too much, and we jump to conclusions without really knowing what the story is. We do that because we are not truly listening to one another. We are simply having a chat with our own minds and listening to what the mind is saying based on our own beliefs and past experiences. This can be called projection—we assume the person is feeling or acting a certain way based on *our own* stories and past experiences. You must become a great listener in order to become more aware of someone's else feelings.

"Seek first to understand, then to be understood."

— STEPHEN R. COVEY

Practice conscious listening. According to Kay Lindahl in her beautiful book *The Sacred Art of Listening,* conscious listening means to suspend assumptions and judgments and listen to understand rather than to agree or believe.

Another way to become a great observer is to amplify awareness by practicing compassion while listening or watching. We know that all of us have experienced suffering in our lives, it is part of life and growth. Before jumping to judgment, can you imagine the pain and wounds that someone else has gone through?

When I teach my classes on Mind-Sets for Happiness, Success, and Health, I tell this story: My friend and I are walking down the street together and we see someone that we both know. My friend says, "That woman is weird, she was so distant when I tried to talk to her during a social gathering." This is just my friend's opinion based on her experience when she met that woman.

I happen to know that woman well, so I say, "She is a wonderful woman; she just lost her mother a few weeks ago, she is having a really rough time."

Do you think you can change your judgment and opinion based on that information? I hope so.

We never know what is really going on with the person who cuts us off in traffic, for example. Maybe he has someone sick in the car, maybe he just got a call his dad had a heart attack. Can you open your mind to the possibilities?

What does this have to do with mind-set? Everything. Change your story and you change your mind-set to a place of love, compassion, and connection. The more you practice this shift, the happier you will be because you will feel more connected with the world. So from this moment on, when you catch yourself in a judgment state, imagine what else could be. Can you see things differently? Is there potential for a different story? Practice compassion and empathy; that is how you will shift your mind-set without effort. I will be covering this topic in more depth in chapter 5.

EXERCISE #3: MEDITATE

"Oh, no, not that, I can't meditate, I can't empty my mind," you may be thinking. I have great news for you: you don't have to empty your mind in order to become an expert in awareness and mind shifting. I define meditation as simply being present with yourself, checking in, feeling your body, breathing deeply.

I find meditation to be a workout for the spirit and the mind. It is one of the greatest ways to create new programming in our subconscious mind, to rewire our brain, and to create peace in any moment. Meditation is the secret of a stress warrior.

There are plenty of studies and data out there proving how much meditation changes our brain, creates better health, and improves well-being, so I won't include any scientific evidence here. I do, however, want to share with you a simple way to start this extremely powerful practice today and change your brain, change your mind, and change your life.

Sit in a comfortable position with your back straight and long. I love sitting on a yoga block with my legs crossed. If that is too hard for you, just sit in a chair or on a high pillow. Set the timer on your phone for 5 to 10 minutes, and start with a few deep breaths. Just sit with the sound of your breath. Be present. Your brain may talk to you about the deadline you have at work, what you are having for lunch, or other mundane stuff. Don't fight it, just go back to your breath. Just accept the thoughts that are coming and let them go, like a gentle breeze. Next, just set your intention for the day. For my intention I say: *I am showing up today with great presence, with love and compassion, with strength and courage. My inner state is peace and joy.*

Create your own mantra, words, intention, and repeat it every day. A key part is whatever you choose to say, say it in the present tense: I am, I have, I do. This way, your mind takes this information as you already are at this moment in time. It connects the conscious mind with the subconscious mind. It becomes your state in the *now*, it is not something that you will obtain in the future. Our minds don't know what is real and what is not, so use the positive force of the words "I am _____" to fully reprogram your subconscious mind and to create the experiences you want.

You can say, "I am showing up today with joy, with courage, with love," or anything you want. Do it every single day, a few times a day, and you will notice that those qualities you call for, to become who you want to become, will turn into your inner state. You must decide how you want to show up. It is an exercise for the mind-brain—awkward maybe in the beginning, but then it becomes part of your subconscious mind. Remember, your conscious mind programs your subconscious mind; use this powerful gift.

I highly recommend that you do this simple practice every morning for 30 days. Commit to it and notice subtle changes in your energy and well-being.

There are many types of meditation. If you want to broaden your knowledge, search for meditation workshops or classes in your area.

Exercise #4: Journal

This is a practice that I love to do at the end of my day or every Sunday. This is an excellent way to evaluate our day, week, month, or year. Based on the challenges or results you had, do an assessment of your thoughts, actions, and behaviors. You must approach this assessment as an observer with love and gentleness, not criticism or judgment. This is a great exercise for awareness. It allows you to gather information about yourself, about actions and behaviors that you need to do more, and others that you need to do less or let go of completely. Since you are reading this book, I assume you are into personal development and personal success. This practice will absolutely help you to keep bettering yourself, to bring you closer and closer to that person you are meant to be. We must manage ourselves in order to become the best version of ourselves.

Get a journal and a cool pen that you love and make the time to write. Create the time; schedule it. Let the thoughts flow, don't correct, don't edit your words. This is a right brain activity, a place to be creative, to express yourself in any form you want. You may want a journal that has blank pages instead of lines, so you can draw, sketch, do whatever you want. Just grab the pen and begin.

For self-assessments, I recommend you start by writing your successful moments of the day or week. For instance, *I handled that difficult client with so much compassion, and I listened with my heart and connected deeply with a friend. I got a new client this week. I remained calm when I was triggered by my partner. I practiced belly breath every day this week.*

Getting into the habit of acknowledging your successes will help you to love yourself more, to appreciate the person you are. The more you do that, the more love you will attract, and you won't need anyone to validate you because you will do it for yourself daily. You are also priming your brain to seek out the positive aspects of life versus the negative. Your optimism muscle will get stronger.

The second part of this exercise is to list things that you believe you could have done better, situations in which you could have made a different choice or spoken different words. Simply write down what you plan to do next time a situation like that arises. Make a commitment with yourself to show up to yourself and others with more brilliance next time. Again, do this part with compassion and understanding. **There is no room for harshness or negative criticism in your journal or in your mind from this day on.**

The Mind-Body Connection

You know well about the body-mind connection—this knowledge is within you. Want to assure yourself? Think about a situation that was scary for you, when you felt your stomach clench. Your breathing was short and your heart was beating like crazy. Yes, your brain is the chief of these body languages. We have an amazing system of hormones, peptides, enzymes, and other biological chemicals that respond to our moment-to-moment demands. If you see a big, scary dog running toward you, for example, within seconds your body will deliver glucose to your muscles, and you will run faster than ever to save your life. This is an easy example to understand the connection between the body and mind because in an emergency situation the body screams.

What about when your body is whispering to you every day that something is off? This is what I call a **silent stressor.** It is there, but it is not in alarm mode yet. This silent stressor may be showing up in the form of a mild headache, a tight chest, lower back pain, constipation, heart palpitations, etc. So maybe it is not so silent after all, right? It depends on if you are listening or not. If you fill your days with noise and distractions, you will not hear what your body is telling you. Reward the voice of your body by choosing to be a super-aware person, and you will hear everything your body has to say. This is one of the reasons making time in the morning for stillness is so important, to connect with yourself and listen to your body.

Is that mild headache telling you that you need to drink more water, eat more healthy foods, or maybe you have a food sensitivity? Do you need to exercise so your neck muscles get stronger? Is the constipation telling you that you are eating foods that are causing blockage? Or are you in so much emotional stress in a relationship that it is shutting down your digestion system? What is your body telling you? Have the courage to ask and listen.

You may say it is a simple physical issue that needs a drug to fix. Sometimes this is true. But what I see mostly are not sick people, people who are carrying an infection or a virus that needs immediate medical treatment. What I see mostly are people with **mediocre levels of energy instead of thriving with vitality and health.** I am talking about the gap in between feeling amazing and being really sick. In that gap lives fatigue, poor sleep, low sex drive, no energy to exercise, mood swings, mild depression, anxiety, headaches, digestive issues, back pain, and an overall feeling of low vitality. Know someone who says they are always tired? Or is that person you?

According to Paul Chek, many of these symptoms could be cured by following a model of six foundation principles. They are our breath, thoughts, hydration, food, movement, and sleep. Imagine what would happen if everybody, before going to see a doctor because of fatigue, followed these principles. Doctors would lose money!

I am not claiming that the symptoms I mentioned above cannot be a sign of an illness. If you follow these six foundation principles and still have symptoms, I recommended that you talk to your doctor. Choose a functional medical doctor if you can; they will focus on the root of the problem, not just on fixing the symptoms.

When you don't feel your best, use a simple checklist to try to pinpoint the issue:

- Am I going through more stress than usual?
- Am I sleeping less than seven to eight hours a night?
- Am I dehydrated?
- Am I eating a poor diet?
- Am I getting enough exercise?
- Am I making time for fun/play?

Once you become aware of one or more of the foundations you might be neglecting, you can manage your routine by make changes like drinking more water, taking more walks, or hiring a nutritionist to help you with your diet.

Fighting Mediocrity

We have created a culture of "feeling okay," "doing okay," or being just "good enough." That has become the status quo; that is mediocrity. Most people have forgotten what feeling great and having high levels of energy is like. Sadly, many people have rarely experienced brilliant health and vitality.

We are wired to feel great, to generate energy all day long, to thrive. When we are not in a state of thriving or high vitality, something is not working well in our body-mind systems. That is why a deep lifestyle assessment is a must before you start popping pills to fix any condition.

So what is your body telling you? You've learned the foundation principles of health (listed above), now complete the following statements. (These statements refer to how you feel in general; sometimes you will be in between. Just make a note.)

WHEN I WAKE UP I FEEL
__ happy, energized.
__ tired, low energy, dragging.

DURING THE DAY MY ENERGY IS
__ stable, I feel great.
__ up and down, and I crash around 3:00 p.m.

IN THE EVENING
__ I am excited to play or share dinner with family and friends.
__ I turn the TV on and check out. I don't have energy for family or friends.

MY BODY FEELS
__ great, I want to move every day.
__ lethargic, full of aches and pains.

I have this mild pain (area) _____, more than three times a week.

MY BRAIN FEELS
__ clear, sharp, focused.
__ foggy, can't concentrate, distracted.

MY MOOD IS
__ happy, positive.
__ unhappy, negative.

Now that you have a better idea how you feel overall, make a connection with each area that you are not feeling your best. What can you do more or less?

How can you amplify your energy, health, and vitality? The first step is awareness; utilize the power of your inner intelligence, your inner voice of wisdom to question why something is not 100 percent. Be your own detective, listen, journal, pay attention, and you will find what is not serving you well.

If you are experiencing poor health and low energy most of the time, consult a holistic health practitioner, like a doctor in naturopath, a holistic lifestyle coach, a skilled acupuncturist, a functional nutritionist, or a functional medical doctor.

Intuition and Divine Guidance

Sometimes you have a gut feeling about something, and you know when you ignore that gut feeling you often regret it. What is that feeling, that intelligence? Some may say it is God speaking to you, your angels whispering in your ears, a download, a sign, a message from the divine. Whatever your belief is, we can't deny that it is a gift we all have at birth, the gift of divine intelligence. We have a body that is highly advanced, with a system that can walk somewhere and instantly feel if it is safe or not. You sense energy in others, their vibration. You feel the energy in the environment. The more you use this gift of feeling your body senses and listening to your inner wisdom, the better you get. Intuition is basically an inner sense you have moment by moment that comes from your divine intelligence, or spirit. To tap into this gift, you just need to pause, become present, and the power is yours. Feel the energy around you and within you.

You don't need to be a religious person to understand a Universal Law that we are not just a physical body, we are energy, we are spiritual beings who connect with another through energy and frequency. Penney Peirce, in her amazing book titled *Frequency*, states: "Your personal vibration—the frequency you hold moment by moment in your body, emotions, and mind—is the most important tool you have for creating and living your ideal life."

Making Your Intuition Stronger

Pause, breathe deeply, create stillness, meditate, and journal. By pausing, breathing, and becoming present you are practicing mindfulness. When you practice mindfulness daily, you will become more intuitive by default. When you meditate for 10 to 15 minutes, you take mindfulness to a deeper level. Meditation is like a workout for the spirit. When you lift weights your muscles get stronger. When you meditate, your awareness and intuition grow stronger. You become spiritually stronger, and that strength will assist you in times of stress and difficulties.

Create a consistent daily practice and start relying on your high divine intelligence. When you connect with the self, you are in full connection with the Force, the Universe, or, maybe for you, God.

Awareness to Enrich Relationships

We must use our awareness toward those around us so we can connect with them on deeper levels—not just our romantic relationship, but all relationships including our friends, our family, and even strangers we meet in a coffee shop.

Let me illustrate this one for you. Let's say I am meeting a friend, and I want to talk about my success, my business, my exciting life. We meet up and I sense that she is sad, or something is off. It would not be appropriate for the best and highest experience of this encounter for me to start talking about myself. I use my awareness to shift the conversation and serve my friend because I am aware that she is not happy.

In a relationship, a great companion to awareness is listening. When we become fully present with someone and listen, we collect data about their inner state and their needs. This information will help us to create greater connections and experiences. Listening is a form of exercise that enhances our awareness. Practice true listening. Great, you say, now what? How do you start using all this knowledge to improve your life? Break it down into three actionable and manageable steps.

1. Start your meditation practice—at least five minutes a day, every morning. Breathe deeply and check the body, your thoughts, and your emotions.
2. Set your intentions for the day. Create a mind-set of success. For example, I end my meditation practice by saying, "I'm showing up

with love, compassion, strength, and grace today. I'm bringing the joy in everything I do, and I am fully present with each person."

This is my daily manifesto; it programs the subconscious mind to follow those instructions. Notice that I use present tense in my sentence. This is really important because it creates a much deeper program into our subconscious mind. If you use "I will" or "I am going to," the mind hears this as a hope, something you might attain in the future, not a deep commitment in the now. Don't underestimate the power in the I AM. If you are trying to change old habits or trying to create new behaviors, this is fundamental.

3. Pay attention to your physical energy and mood throughout the day. Did it change? When? Why? What was the trigger? Do you need water or food? Did someone say something that made your body contract? This is how you will develop a tremendous level of awareness and deepen your knowledge about yourself.

This is not hard science. Just slow down, do one task at the time, connect with others, be fully present, and pay attention. Listen, speak slowly, breathe deeply, and your whole well-being will smile.

Journal Time

Think about the four main areas in your life—career/job, relationships, finances, health/fitness—as you respond to the following questions.

- The systems in your life that are working great are…
- Do you have any systems that are not working?
- Why aren't they working and how would you like to change them?
- What behaviors or patterns do you want to change? Why?

P.S. When saying or writing your new state of mind and being, use the present tense: I AM

Two

BELIEFS

"A Belief is a thought in your Mind."

— DR. JOSEPH MURPHY

A belief is a thought that we think over and over. A belief is the core and root of our feelings, behaviors, and emotions. Beliefs can also be viewed as systems we have in our life that rule every choice we make. A belief also rules our perception of ourselves, others, and the world around us.

Beliefs work like a rudder in a boat; they give us direction and help us make decisions. A belief can also be viewed as just an opinion and we are free to change it anytime. That is freedom.

The power of change lives within our beliefs. Our beliefs work like lenses on your camera; you will see the same scene differently with each type of lens. Defining our beliefs and understanding how they are affecting all of our decisions and experiences is the key for change, evolution, and transformation. Since this book is about how we can make changes in order to create an extraordinary life, this chapter may be one of the most important chapters of this book because what you believe about yourself, life, and the Universe will attract people, situations, and circumstances that will match that belief. It is a Universal Law.

Dr. Joe Dispenza, best-selling author of *Evolve Your Brain* among others, says in his book *Breaking the Habit of Being Yourself:*

> *If your thoughts determine your reality, and you keep thinking the same thoughts, then you will continue to produce the same reality day after day. Thus, your internal thoughts and feelings exactly match your external life, because it is your outer reality—with all of its problems, conditions, and circumstances—that is influencing how you are thinking and feeling in your inner reality.*

The key to freedom lives in our power to change our beliefs.

Let's Take The Hero's Journey

In order for you to change your life from this moment on, you must take responsibility for what you have created so far. If you haven't done this yet, keep reading because it is my intention that with deeper work and creative thinking, you will get to that by the time you finish this book, hopefully after reading this chapter. Believe me, when you take responsibility for your thoughts, emotions, and behaviors, you hold a superpower, the superpower of energy and creation that will allow you to become the person you are designed to be. This is how you become the super YOU, the best version of yourself. This is your hero's journey.

The hero's journey isn't a journey without fear and it isn't a journey without pain and tough challenges. The hero's journey is a path of courage, which you will need in order to move through fear; it is a path of passion, which is required to give you the fuel you will need in order to get up when things are falling apart; it is a path of grit, which you will need to endure in times of difficulty; and it is a path of strength, which you will need when you have to make a hard decision. With courage, passion, grit, and strength, you can handle anything because it is the path of your purpose, your dream river. It is the path that you travel until you leave this physical world, and when you do, you will leave screaming, "Woohoo!

21

I did it, I lived my best, I lived my full potential." That is my wish for all of us.

How Did You Get Here?

Now that we have decided that you are the superhero of your own life, I am going to help you understand how you got here—how your beliefs brought you here and how they created your experiences, both great ones and hard ones. I am going to show you how some of your beliefs are not even yours, but they are still ruling your life. It is time for you to take charge; you are holding the key to happiness, success, and freedom. Don't ever forget that.

My Hero's Journey

I was blessed by being born in Brazil in 1970. I am a Libra, if you care about horoscopes.

I grew up in an average middle-class family. My mom was the bread-winner, and my dad could not hold a job. Mom was always bailing him out until the day she grew tired of it and got a divorce. It was not all pretty for us, but that is another story.

Mom provided everything I needed. She made sure my grand-mother and I had good food on the table, clothes, shelter, and security. Considering those are our prime needs, we had everything. While Mom was super busy working full-time and having fun dating (she was only 32 years old when she got divorced), my grandmother was giving me the love I needed in order to be a healthy child and adult. Even though my grandmother gave me tons of love—yes, she spoiled me—I wanted more. I wanted attention from my mom, and I wanted to have a father who participated in my life. I wanted a father who played sports with me, took me camping, someone who did not watch TV all day while I was bored to death in my room.

I did not have parents who played with their kids all weekend. I had parents who watched TV all day on a sunny Sunday. They did the best they could, the best they knew. It was a different era, a different culture from today and the United States.

Being bored and lonely was actually a blessing. It was a blessing because it pushed me to want a different life. Boredom got me to grow up with a dissatisfaction with and deep curiosity about life. My boredom and my loneliness were my gifts. They drove me to have the courage to move to the United States in 1996. I could not accept that life was meant to be boring and mediocre. I saw people around me living the life that was designed for them, not the life they truly designed. They followed the crowd rather than taking the lead. I was not a crowd follower, which made life hard for me because I was not surrounded by people who felt like me. I was a fish out of water. In fact, I wrote an essay with that title when I was in the third grade. Something felt wrong, off, but I could not define what it was at that young age. I moved to the United States when I was 26, and I was a very young 26. My world changed the day I landed in San Diego. It changed because everything was unknown. My hero's journey had begun.

What gave me the courage to move to a new country without speaking one word of English? A deep desire for change. That is the secret, the key that opens the magic portal of transformation and creative living. The desire for change needs to be burning inside your chest, like nothing else. You don't need to know *how* you will change initially, you just need to know you want to make changes in your life. You must get to that moment of full awareness and with a vulnerable heart admit, "This is not working."

We have built a society that needs answers, precise goals, and plans; it needs to know what the future holds. If you wait for that knowing, you will never change.

I will tell you right now, if you are a control freak who needs to know what the future holds for you in detail, you must drop that belief right now. You will not enjoy this ride at all if you need to know everything. That will take you away from living in the present and make you give up easily. So right now I ask you to be courageous and trust that once you know what you want, even if all you know right now is that you must change, the Universe will support you. Having faith in a higher power will really help you in this journey. Even if you don't believe in anything, can you believe that you hold the power of creating what you want? That is enough for now.

The hero's journey is about dropping beliefs that don't support you anymore. I call these beliefs stones that you carry in your backpack. They make your pack heavy, and you must travel light so you can get to where you're going faster. Who put those stones there? Are you ready to let go of some of them?

How Beliefs Get Programmed in our Mind

What drives your behaviors, actions, and emotions every day, every moment is your subconscious mind. To recap, your subconscious mind never stops working, even when you are sleeping. It is constantly processing information that is put there by your conscious mind. You may be more aware of what you put there in the present moment by practicing awareness. But what about the old programs you are still carrying around that were installed there when you were, say, five years old? How do we access those beliefs, evaluate them, and then change if they are not in alignment with the way we want to live our lives?

First, how do we end up with beliefs that we did not create ourselves? When we are born, we come into this world with a fully open mind, open to experiences and teachings. We have no ability to judge, to filter what we want to listen to or learn. We absorb everything when we are little kids. We listen, feel energy, obey, and act as we are told or as we see. Our parents or caretakers are the first people in our lives to show us a model of living. We start mirroring their traits, their ways to deal with stress, with family, with each other, and especially the way they relate to us. We learn the language and the emotions. For instance, were your parents affectionate with each other and with you? Did you get hugs? Did you learn to trust others because they were always there for you? Were you held when you cried and had needs? Did you feel loved? Or were you neglected or ignored? Did you feel left out by your siblings?

Did you get teased a lot? Did you feel during childhood that something was wrong with you?

All these aspects of the environment and the connections we had with our caretakers become the first experiences in our lives; they can be loving, joyful experiences or they can be sad, traumatizing, dysfunctional, and harsh experiences. At early ages, when we have no idea how to cope with challenges, we shut down and we distract ourselves, that way we suppress the suffering. For example, when I was six years old, my mom had a baby. His name was Marcos. He was born with a mal-formation of his skull and needed surgery to fix it. At five months old he had the surgery, but he did not survive. I am sure my parents' suffering was traumatizing to them. I have no memory of those times. It is like I had a Force that protected me from all that hurt because it was not going to serve me. At the same time, I know that experience caused great suffering to my parents, and I am not sure how they expressed their grief other than having a very unhappy marriage and divorcing three years after that. Were their emotions projected onto me? Possibly. I watched my mom shut down for years, never expressing a lot of emotions. That information and experience were being programmed into my subconscious mind. I had not just a model to follow, but also an insecurity about not feeling loved. I am sure many of you had that feeling around your mother or father. Most people deal or have dealt with insecurities, the source of feeling like, "I am not good enough." This "I am not good enough" complex comes from very early experiences and continues during school years. We all remember those tough times in school, don't we?

The other sources of our subconscious beliefs come from authority figures like our teachers, religious leaders, family members, mentors, or older siblings. And of course, there are the other kids. I am sure you remember at least one kid who called you fat, ugly, boring, annoying, or simply did not let you play with the cool kids. That leaves a mark on us. The rejection mark—who does not feel rejected or fear rejection? We all do.

So we make it through middle school and then reach high school when our egos are fully formed and we go hard on forming opinions about ourselves and others. That comes from our need to form our identity. Rejection can be a big one here, when we have our first crush on a boy or girl, we want to fit in with the cool or smart kids, we want to be invited to the rich kid's party. When our needs are not met, we get upset and believe we are not cool enough, rich enough, thin enough, pretty enough, smart enough, sexy enough—you get the idea. All those opinions and thoughts repeated over and over become our BELIEFS.

It does not stop here. We go to college, perhaps fall in love deeply for the very first time, have amazing sex with that person who makes us feel that connection we have been pining for our whole life. We think we have found the love of our life—some of you probably did and are still with that person, lucky you. But in many cases, like myself, we lost that love. That connection that makes us feel so alive, so great about ourselves, and so loved is gone. What do we do, in most cases? We say to ourselves, "I will never find this kind of love again" or "I will never open my heart again" or "I will only have flings" and other stories. Be careful with the stories. Stories are just organized thoughts. Because emotions charge our thoughts, as we will discuss later in the book, they become a belief that becomes part of our code of living. You put that code into your subconscious mind by using your conscious mind. Maybe you wrote in your journal, told all your friends, and spent many nights crying to reinforce those stories. You anchored that belief deep into your body, mind, and soul. It will be there forever unless you move it. And you can move it, anytime you decide to.

By now you should have a good understanding that all your experiences, emotions, and perceptions formed your beliefs, the codes that rule your decisions, choices, and patterns every day, every moment.

"I Got Over My Childhood Experiences, But…"

When I coach my clients on how to be successful, I am basically searching for, with their help, what areas are blocked because of their own limiting and disempowering beliefs. It gets tricky when they have assured themselves that they have worked out all their issues from early age. They did therapy, yoga, meditation, energy work, etc. However, based on their outcomes and low levels of satisfaction with romance, work, money, body, or any other area, I know they are not living their highest potential because they are still carrying around deep-seated beliefs.

Many times we "resolve" issues in a very intellectual way. In other words, we may simply say to ourselves, "I am not going to feel this way anymore. Look at what I have: money, expensive cars, I travel, I have friends, and I am successful. I got it all, I proved I can." But still, many with all that material stuff feel deeply unfulfilled, unhealthy, and unhappy. That is what our intellectual minds can drive us to do. Work hard, use willpower, sacrifice your health and well-being, push through it, and have it all.

I am all for working hard, but we can't lose sight of the meaning, why we are working hard, and what for. Otherwise, hard work is just a distraction by being busy all the time, so we don't do the real hard work, the inner work. The work that requires us to sit, to get honest with ourselves, to really face our fears head on, our heartbreaks, our wounds that are still not healed, our anger that still lives inside because someone betrayed us. We need to address the feeling of "not good enough" as part of our inner work. The distractions of working 12-plus hours a day, shopping sprees, social nights, and relationships do not change that deep belief because the subconscious mind never got a new program. That state of being is still the same, even though the external world looks different. That is what too much intellectuality can do.

The evidence of whether you have truly changed a belief is very simple: look at the results and outcomes in your life. Do you love what you see, do you love what you feel? Are you living with peace of mind? If you answered yes to all, continue reading to simply strengthen your beliefs and teach this model to others. If you said no, read, study, and embody the concepts of this book. Most importantly, take the time to do the journal part at the end of each chapter. Only by allowing your beliefs and emotions to emerge will you transform your life. Remember the first chapter? Awareness is a prerequisite to change. We can't heal what we don't feel. Give yourself permission to go within and change whatever you want to change. The beauty of being an adult is that we decide what we want to believe, we choose our systems and philosophies of life. We decide the environment we want to be a part of and the kind of people we want to surround ourselves with. We don't need to follow our father's belief about money, our mother's belief about how we should have security by having a nine to five job. What beliefs are you living that are not yours and that are not working? It's time to look at them.

Road Map To Identifying Limiting and Disempowering Beliefs

You can start identifying your own limiting beliefs by doing a life assessment. Ask yourself these questions:

- Do I have a job that I love and fulfills me?
- Am I making the money I want?
- Do I have a loving partnership/relationship?
- Do I love the city I live in?
- Do I love my living environment?
- Do I have rich friendships?
- Am I healthy?
- Do I have a life that feels joyful, playful, and abundant?

You can go on and on with questions that will help you to find the underlying subconscious beliefs. You can think in four areas: career/work, relationships, finances, and health/fitness. Those are the four main areas in our lives, the ones we are constantly working on or ignoring. Ignore one of this areas, and you know the result won't be positive.

In the next section I will be sharing how, through conscious choices, you can reprogram your subconscious mind.

My Story-Belief About Money

About the time I turned 40 (five years ago), I started having a crisis. This is the time for a crisis, right? A midlife crisis means we don't now fully who we are or our purpose in life. The crisis comes from us wanting our life to be different. I did love turning 40, and I will say the 40s have been the best years for me so far. I call it the decade of no more b.s. We either get life or we don't. It is the period when many change careers, go back to school, get divorced, remarry, take a year off to travel, etc. It is the time, I believe, that many of us realize that we have lived half of our good years already and we don't have time to waste. It is a big reality check, I have found.

So I did my check-in and had a crisis, realizing that I had great education with more than twenty years of experience in my field, was working at one of the best health clubs, around the most knowledgeable trainers and coaches, I was doing a lot of continuing education, reading books, doing therapy to improve myself, I was getting super healthy—and I was broke! I was always struggling with money, never had enough to travel, to have nice dinners with friends, to buy nice gifts, or to buy clothes that I wanted. I was always worried about every dollar. But at the same time, I was in denial that I had a problem. I would not look at my online bank statements, I would not plan my finances, and when I did something to make more money, it was based on willpower and fear. This was a place of shame and embarrassment for me. How could I be forty years old, intelligent, driven, live in one of the best towns in the United States, have a great education, be a good person, and be always broke? That was my midlife crisis.

Those were moments of tears for me. When I surrendered to that state, I realized that I was stuck, that for more than five years I had made the same amount of money per year. I surrendered and accepted that I had an area in my life that was stale, that needed some major rethinking and transformation. I looked at the issue of money head on. What I was really looking at was my fear, my limited belief that "I was not designed to be rich," that there was something wrong with me, that I did not have the education to make money or know-how to be financially successful. I believed I was a different type of person, that I did not belong to the "rich group." I would be like most people in my family, I would always make enough to pay the bills, living paycheck to paycheck. My limiting beliefs had created my money outcome.

Years ago, before I broke the code of how my subconscious beliefs about money were sabotaging me, I did all the intellectual stuff to change my state. I read Brian Tracy Napoleon Hill's books and wrote in my journal how much money I was going to make and my goals to bring me financial fulfillment. Well, none of that worked. Why? Because I took a shortcut; I focused on these external actions of making vision boards, writing positive affirmations on sticky notes, and reading books on success. Nothing changed except the fact that I was more irritated and frustrated. After all, I was "doing everything right," or so I thought.

I am sharing this with you because I am sure some of you will relate to my story. Have you tried to lose weight many times and got no results? Or maybe you did and then after a while you gained all the weight back? Or maybe you got super motivated to make some changes in your life because you attended a Tony Robbins seminar, and a week later, you were back in the mud, stuck again.

We all have failed, and what a gift failure can be because it gives us information about what works and what does not. We improve after each failure. I see failure as just a roadblock toward success. Many people see failure as a setback. I don't because I don't believe we move backward as long as we continue on our path of success and excellence. If you choose to freeze in fear and quit, then I will say that is the ultimate failure that will set you back.

Let's get clear about something right away. The moment you decide to up level your life to a higher standard or a higher potential, you will have moments of failure, just know it is part of the journey. If you are not failing, you are not working on your success. You are holding yourself back and living with an illusion that you can live your best life without failure. Save yourself from frustration and stress and make friends right now with failure. Never look at failure as a weakness, look at it with the eyes of a warrior and learn from it. Learn what went wrong, what you can do differently next time, and move on. Failure is a teacher.

How I Changed My Relationship With Money

I can't recall the moment because it was a buildup of many moments that taught me how to change my own relationship with money.

To make a long story short, I first realized that my subconscious programming about money came from my parents and my environment. As I mentioned, my mom was the provider until she remarried and my stepfather helped us. He paid for my college, which I am so grateful for. They were both hard workers, paid all the bills on time, and never had any debt. We had a house paid off in the suburbs of Saõ Paulo and even a small house on the beach. We had fresh food every day, nice clothes, and a good life.

We did all the things that people at our income level did. We hung out at the beach and other places where people at similar income levels were. That was all I knew. When I mentioned that I wanted a house on a different beach where I thought the cool people were, they would say, "That is only for rich people." I would say, "Let's travel." "That is for rich people," they reiterated. Or sometimes they did not need to say anything, their looks gave it all: "That is not for us." I used to ask, "Why don't we hang out with Walter?" a rich friend they had. Their answer: "We can't, he is rich and we can't afford doing the things he does," which I agreed with, that was true. He went for expensive dinners, had fancy cars, and took international vacations; however, it was how they spoke that was the issue. It made me truly believe that we were different.

Today, looking back, I have this conclusion: we had a life that was completely separated from the riches. Rich people were different than us, as if they belonged to another category, had a different gene, special gifts, and special educational degrees. This created a belief in me by default. I believed that I could never be rich because I was not like them. This had been my limiting and disempowering belief for most of my life, therefore, I always had a poor relationship with money.

To top that off, when I went to pursue my physical education degree, after failing in engineering school for over a year, my mom said to me that I would never make money with that type of college degree. I remember that moment. After she said that, the next day I got a job as a swim coach in a small swim academy. So there was already this defiant part of me that was saying, "Watch me." But here you can see how having moments like that, when someone with authority whom we love and respect, like a parent, can plant a belief in our subconscious mind, and unless we take the time to retrieve those memories, we don't unlock those beliefs in order to change them. I changed my story with money, and today I have a great relationship with it, where money is always abundant and my life has improved in many ways.

Change your story, change your life.

Emotional Energy

Changing my relationship with money did not happen overnight. Like I said, it did not change by writing down my goals and making a vision board. It did not change until I charged those new thoughts about money with emotion.

Emotion is how you feel about something. For instance, what feelings do you experience when you think about money, success, and health? Excitement? Fear? Shame? Emotions and feelings are responses in your body based on your beliefs. This is a crucial step toward anchoring your new beliefs. Think about how your old beliefs got so deep within you—it's because they had great emotional charge, especially the ones that came from difficult experiences like trauma and hard losses. Those moments with strong emotional charge are always remembered. Everyone in the United States, for example, remembers exactly where they were at the moment that 9/11 happened.

If it took emotional charge to carve those beliefs in you, it will take emotional charge to create new ones. The cool thing now is that you get to choose. It is not happening by default anymore, you are in full control of what goes in and what goes out.

Dr. Dispenza wrote an amazing book titled *You Are the Placebo,* which is about how we use our minds to change our state of being. He shares incredible stories of people who had incurable diseases or lived with chronic pain, and by using focused meditation where they learned how to elevate their emotions, they were able to change their brain and change the expression of their genes. They were able to turn their genes off, putting the disease or pain back into a dormant state. They had to convince their subconscious minds that their bodies were healed, that they were pain free or disease free. They transformed their lives. This is the power of visualization. You tap into the emotions of having what you want, like it is your new reality.

This is the concept of the Law of Attraction. In the movie *The Secret*, they failed in sharing this ultimate secret of emotional charge or an elevated emotion. That is why so many people like myself had vision boards with pretty pictures of money, mansions, and exotic places to travel that were just collecting dust because they didn't do much to manifest new results. That was just an action without emotion; it was empty.

Now, I am not saying don't have your goals written down or a vision board. Have it all! Have sticky notes everywhere, books, quotes, anything that will reflect the new life you want to create. Have a vision board, but make sure you spend a few minutes looking at the board every day and elevating the emotions to a place where you already have all you want. Add the most powerful ingredient, emotional energy, and your life will transform in miraculous ways. I changed my relationship with money by visualizing what I wanted, believing that it was possible, and feeling like I had it all already. I was energizing the dream with my emotions. I created a new state of mind. As Dr. Dispenza states:

NEW EMOTIONS = NEW PROGRAM
Belief + Actions + Emotional Energy = New State of Mind, New State of Being

The subconscious mind does not know the difference between what is real and what is not. Don't ever forget this.

Just to recap before I end this chapter

Changing our beliefs starts with a declaration like, "Enough." We must decide what beliefs we need to let go of and why. And the moment we bring new thoughts that will form the new belief, we must energize those thoughts with emotions. By defining your goals or dreams, short term or long term, you are able to define your new beliefs that will align with those goals. Not knowing what you want or where you want to go will make it much harder to design your new belief system.

Keep it simple. Maybe you just want to work on your health goals right now because you are done being overweight, or you are done not having energy. Or you may be tired of being broke, like I was, so your goals are to create financial security. Don't try to work on every aspect of your life at the same time. One small change, one breakthrough will guide you to the next, then to the next. All you need to see is where you are now and where you want to go next. So just get started and the journey will take a life force itself, and the more focused you become about what you want, the more guidance you will receive. We will discuss focus in chapter 6.

Journal Time

Take a few deep breaths and become present. Ponder the following questions and write down your answers freely and honestly.

- What areas in your life do you want to improve or grow? (Remember the four areas are career, relationships, finances, and health/fitness.)
- What limiting beliefs do you have that are keeping you stuck in one or more areas?
- Where did those beliefs come from?
- List at least three actions you will be taking starting now to anchor new beliefs.
- List one to three habits or behaviors that you are eliminating from your life.

- How will your life change by having these new beliefs? Feel the emotions behind your description.
- In the present tense, write a paragraph stating your new thinking.
  Example: I am living a life filled with health, wealth, love, and joy. I am fully capable to create financial freedom. I am powerful, I am courageous, and I am a divine being.

Read your statement every day, or anytime you feel the old thoughts slipping back into your mind.

Three

CONFIDENCE

*"My confidence comes from the daily grind—
training my butt off day in and day out."*

— *HOPE SOLO*

I talked about beliefs for a whole chapter, the thoughts that you collect every day that rule your actions, behaviors, and emotions. This chapter is about creating a deep belief so that you can amplify and strengthen your confidence muscle. You will learn what confidence is, how to cultivate it, and how to bring it into your life every day and use it consciously when doubts, fear, and stress arise.

Simply telling yourself every day, "I am confident" as part of your positive thinking is a great start, but it needs to become authentic in order to help you take bold actions that are required for your success. You need to own the emotion of confidence, feel it in every cell of your body. Confidence is the feeling of deep trust in yourself that you will learn and figure out whatever you need in the process of pursuing your goals.

In order to fully understand confidence, we must understand fear. They are not opposites, fear never disappears because you have confidence and courage. But with authentic confidence and courage you can overcome fear, you make fear smaller, you don't attach to it, you still see it, name it, and feel it. You make friends with fear and use it to charge your confidence. We'll delve much more into fear in chapter 6.

So how do we strengthen this muscle named confidence? You are about to find out.

Confidence is the core muscle of any achievement.

There is No Lack of Confidence

I don't want you to believe everything I say. It is my hope that this book sparks a deep curiosity in you to learn more about your own power to achieve anything you want in this life. However, I will ask you to believe this: **you already have everything you need to succeed in your life.** You have confidence inside you, ready to get amplified in order to fuel your life's vision into manifestation.

Do yourself a favor and eliminate this sentence forever: "I don't have confidence." I never want to hear you saying that because it is not true, you were born with confidence, no one gives you confidence or takes confidence away from you. Certainly, life's early challenges can dim the light of your confidence so you don't see it or feel it, but because you don't see it or feel it does not mean it is not there. It is and it is waiting for you to touch it and use as your superpower.

Since the topic of this book is about creating mental fitness, I will refer to confidence as a muscle in that it grows stronger as you work it or it atrophies if you don't do any work to stress it. I use the word stress because in order to grow anything you must provide stimulus, or stress. Stress gets a very bad reputation because it gets abused and mismanaged. Stress is an amazing thing that helps us to change, to grow, and to create the life we want.

In sports physiology terms, when you go to the gym and lift heavy weights to get stronger or build muscles, you are stressing each muscle tissue, even creating micro tears in the muscle fiber. In fact, while at the gym, you are getting weaker. The miracle happens afterward, while you eat and rest. When you consume a nutritious meal to replace basic raw material, like high-quality carbohydrates, healthy fats, and grass-fed/pasture-raised animal proteins, you are allowing your body to repair the muscles and promote what is called overcompensation. Overcompensation means that the body makes your muscle fibers thicker so you can push extra weights next time, that way you can cause a higher demand, or more stress, so you continue progressing. You get stronger, better at your sport, faster, and you get better at dealing with the physical and mental stress. In other words, a hard, intense workout does not scare you anymore as it did in the beginning of your training. I will be covering stress in detail in chapter 5.

I use this analogy in relation to your confidence muscle because I want you to start getting the concept that stress is great. To have a fit body and a fit mind for success, you must become really good at handling stress. It makes you a warrior, one who does not avoid stress but one who can stand strong with it and thrive. To be a fit warrior who can handle any stress, you need to have confidence.

Still, you might be saying, "Really, Alex, I don't have confidence in my life." And I will say back to you, is that really true? Here is a test.

Look back at your life, maybe as far back as middle or high school. Did you play sports? Did you participate in a school play, dance, or any other performance? Did you have to get a job to support your family or yourself?

I want you to dig deep right now and say out loud at least two to three achievements that you've had in your past. Whatever they were, they required confidence with at least an "I can do this" attitude. You practiced, you took actions to get better, you learned more, and you made choices daily that got you mentally and/or physically fit for that challenge.

Think of someone in your life who overcame great challenges. Or think of Nelson Mandela, Jim Carrey, Bethany Hamilton, Sylvester Stallone, Viktor Frankl, and other remarkable people in history who overcame extreme challenges and are role models today.

You've got confidence, my friend. I will keep telling you that until you see it and feel it. Stop the self-centered chat in your mind right now thinking everyone's got confidence but you.

If you say you are lacking the belief of confidence in certain areas, good, you are a normal human being; we all lack confidence at times. We all have areas where we show up with more confidence than others. Some people are masters in making money but lack skills on social aspects. Some are great connectors, lovers but don't have confidence in making money. Some people are super successful in their careers but have very low confidence when it comes to intimate relationships.

I have been a very athletic person my whole life. Learning sports came easily for me, I have always been very good at learning any movement or exercise with a little practice. That talent built confidence in me. As an adult, I took up bike racing, running races, swim meets, and was always able to build a very fit body. I was great being fit and helping people to get fit. I still help people to transform their physical fitness.

Now, to return to my story in chapter 2, when it comes to dealing with money and creating financial abundance, the confidence was not there. I was an avoider. I had the attitude that everything was just going to work out, not really putting forth actions to make things great in that area. I made enough every month to just pay the bills, and some months I could not pay all the bills, so I used credit cards, thinking, I can just pay later, money will come. Does this sound familiar?

After years on that same path, stories were repeating themselves, and I was always broke. I realized my confidence in making money was low or not existent because I did not do anything to get better at it. Confidence does not come out of nowhere. It comes with awareness, as we discussed in the first chapter, then it comes with the desire to make a change. Confidence gets cultivated by three elements:

1. Practice
2. Actions with Purpose
3. Self-Assessment

You don't just get the feeling of confidence overnight. Think of these three elements as exercises that strengthen confidence, that must be performed every single day.

Russ Harris, author of the book *The Confidence Gap*, says it well: **"The actions of confidence come first; the feelings of confidence come later."** The misconception about confidence is exactly what might be stopping you from doing what you love. You are waiting to get up one day and feel confident. Forget it, it won't happen. Start by owning what you want, learning what needs to be done, taking actions, and then you will start to feel confident.

I want you to fully understand what builds your confidence and what kills it. Let's take a closer look at the three elements that build confidence.

The Confidence Builders
1. Practice
What area of your life you do want to upgrade your confidence in? It might be career, relationships, communication, public speaking, health, fitness, etc. Whatever it is, once you decide to master confidence in that area, all you need to do is define what it takes to be great at it. For instance, in the communication arena, you need to be great at it to enhance your relationships, for work, and even for emotional or mental health. Have a list of what skills you need to develop more and learn new ones in order to have strategic actions that will help you to build confidence. The word at this stage of defining what you want to improve is START. Just start without worrying about the hows and what ifs. Stop that voice that may say you cannot, you should not, you are not. Just start, maybe now is the best time.

Pause and identify what you want. Make a list of daily practices you need to implement in order to get better. Remember, to master anything in life we must practice. Practice every day is like going to the gym to get stronger. Your body changes, your energy changes, you become more motivated to change your habits in order to be healthier. **Practice builds the confidence muscle.** If you are not sure what practices or strategies you need, hire a coach who can support you. Find the people who have the qualities you want and ask them how they did it. Learn what their habits and practices are. These people are a few miles ahead of you; ask them to guide you.

Discipline

How do we make new beliefs and practices to stick? You may be thinking by now of all those times you tried to lose weight, save money, or had a relationship that did not last. It worked for a while then you went back to old patterns and behaviors. Was it lack of discipline? Do you say to yourself, "I don't have the discipline to create the change I want"? What you lack is not discipline, what you might lack is clarity and deep desire. You are not sure what you want, or if you do, your desire needs to be amplified. Clarity and desire are the fuel for discipline. Discipline, just like confidence, is a mental muscle; it gets stronger when worked daily, when you practice over and over, especially during the times you don't feel like doing it. But if you are trying too hard, if you are relying on willpower all the time, discipline will not be sustainable.

If you read any books about success, you read about how discipline is a requirement to achieve any goal. Discipline can be defined as doing what you need to do when you don't feel like doing it. You do the work no matter what.

Many people don't like the word "discipline" because it relates to punishment. You may have had a strict father or mother who disciplined you with harsh rules, and you rebelled against the word discipline. Discipline for some means rigidity and rules. But a little bit of rigidity in areas where we are slacking off that it is causing us delay in our success is a great thing. I like to replace "rigidity" with "strong": make a habit or a practice strong, not rigid. Rules serve us well. If you are trying to lose weight, you need to set some rules around food, exercise, and sleep. The same goes if you want to buy a new house and save money. Or you want to start a business and need time to research and learn about marketing and strategies. Anything you want in life will require time, effort, and energy. You will need to give away something in order to create time and energy for something else. That requires discipline and the implementation of new habits that align with your new goals.

All my friends and many clients tell me how disciplined I am because of my morning rituals, my sleep schedule, the food I eat, and my exercise routines. The thing is that all these habits feel natural to me. They are habits that meet my daily essential needs in order for me to have a successful day. Accomplishing these rituals daily are easy for me, for the most part. There are some days that I need to rely on my discipline muscle, like if I am committed to run three times a week and there is a day I don't want to run—it happens. I don't negotiate with myself, I just get out and do it. You must commit to yourself and to your goals and do the work no matter what.

Without discipline, we would just do the things that we feel like doing. Most of the time we make decisions with emotions. If we relied only on our emotions to achieve our goals, we would not climb very far. **Clear goals are the anchor of discipline.**

The ONE Thing, a book by Gary Keller and Jay Papasan, talks about the truth behind extraordinary results. This is what they say about discipline:

> *Contrary to what most people believe, success is not a marathon of disciplined action. Achievement does not require you to be a full-time disciplined person where your every action is trained and where control is the solution to every situation. Success is actually a short race—a sprint fueled by discipline just long enough for habit to kick in and take over.*

Basically, this means rely on discipline until your new habit becomes strong and natural. Keller and Papasan also say, "Success is about doing the right thing, not about doing everything right." This falls under actions with purpose.

Master your habits that serve your life's vision, that make you master discipline without creating rigidity or rules that can't ever be broken—that is stressful (the bad kind of stress), not realistic.

Researchers say it takes about 66 days to establish a new habit. So choose that habit, mark your calendarddd, and practice it! No room for negotiation. As the Nike slogan says, just do it.

2. ACTIONS WITH PURPOSE

Now that you know that a daily practice is a must to succeed in having confidence, the next step is to become very clear about what actions will help you the most.

We live in a world that bombards us 24/7 with too much information and different concepts in diet, exercise, health, money, and so on. It can be overwhelming to decide what approach to take. Here's a secret: keep it simple. "Master the fundamentals" is a philosophy we use in sports, and the same can be applied to success. Keep it simple, focus on the aspects that really matter, and do them well.

What I mean by this concept is, for example, if you want to build confidence in your body image, feel sexier, get leaner, and be fit, you must eat a healthy diet. Eat real and fresh foods, that is all. Don't buy processed food, junk food, or anything that comes in a package with ingredients that you can't even read because it is not real food. And avoid all the genetically modified foods. Buy local as much as you can, support the farmers in your community, and you will get the best foods.

Go to the gym, hire a trainer who can teach you the fundamentals in strength training, like squats, lunges, pulling, pushing, and core exercises. Nothing fancy, just the fundamentals, then they will tell you how often to do it and how much to do it. You follow the instructions. Once you master the fundamentals for four to six weeks, you go back and get a new routine based on your progression from those fundamental exercises. It is that simple.

But simple does not mean easy, right? I am not giving you a recipe for easy. I am sharing a simple recipe for success that involves hard work at times, energy, and effort.

The only reason it isn't easy at first is because you are modifying your current habits and incorporating new ones. We are emotionally attached to our current habits, so letting go of old habits touches our emotions, that is why it can he hard. Our habits are addicting, that is why a trainer, a life coach, or a mentor can accelerate your process of achieving your goals. If you want something bad enough, you make it happen.

Actions with purpose means you focus on one to two things a day that are the most important for you to improve the areas you want. Don't fill your list of actions with five or more things; you will fail and feel discouraged. Focus on one action at a time and be successful at it, master it. That success will fuel you to take the next challenge and succeed again. You train yourself in how to be a great achiever. The strategies will be the same for anything you want to achieve.

How to Choose Your Actions without Struggle
For each action you define, ask yourself, "Is this action in perfect alignment with my purpose or goal?" If the answer is yes, great. Start practicing it. If it is a maybe, don't sweat it, just put it at the bottom of your list and assess the next task.

Here's an example: my goal is that I want to get better at finances, be more confident about money, and feel that money is abundant and I can create it.

Actions with purpose:

- Hire a financial advisor.
- Save a small amount of money every month toward a retirement account (I started with $150 a month).
- Create a budget for dinners out, clothes, and play.
- Learn how many clients I need a month to pay all the bills and myself.

Daily practices:

- Track in a small notebook all my daily expenses.
- Meditate on abundance. Money is just energy, it flows. No fear around it.
- Be generous with money.

Notice that my actions and practices are few and very simple. Just doing those things daily built my confidence around money. They helped me to believe that I have the ability to create as much as I want, that money will always be available. It also built my confidence in controlling the money versus letting the money control me. This strategy eliminated the stress I had around money.

Not doing something that we know in our hearts we should do is one of the greatest sources of daily stress. I call it a silent stressor; you may not talk about it or see it, but it is always there, consuming your energy.

Not Being Clear about Your Actions

If you find that you are not clearly defining your actions with purpose, then you need a better understanding of what you want and what skills you need. There are many areas in our lives for which we may need to seek help beyond books, seminars, or online courses. Sometimes we need direct attention from a skilled coach, a counselor, or a therapist. Working with a professional can save us years of struggles sometimes. I have worked with many coaches over the years and I still do.

I remember when I was having a lot of difficulties communicating with a partner, I decided to see a coach, and what she taught me was so valuable. I learned how to be a very effective communicator, how to speak my truth from my heart, and how to stay on top of any issues. She gave me a few things to work on every day during conversations with my partner—those were my daily practices. She gave me books to read and assignments—those were my actions with purpose. Working with a coach can boost our confidence and decreases stress instantly. This is because we are being pro-active when we hire a coach and move something from our should list to our must list. We feel in control of a situation that before we probably felt like was controlling us. The key is to take advantage of that confidence boost and start practicing right way so that confidence is sustained and amplified.

You will never succeed alone. **Asking for help is key for growth and success.** Working with a coach saves you time, energy, and money! They've already done the work that you are learning about. They have developed strategies that will help you get there faster. They can bounce ideas back and forth with you so you feel your approach is sound. They see things in a different way than you do. When you're not wasting time, you become an extremely effective human being, always acting with purpose.

Today I work with a life coach myself. He helps me tremendously in areas where I am not sure how to proceed. He brings me back to the simple concepts.

"No one succeeds alone. No one."

— GARY KELLER

3. SELF-ASSESSMENT

Self-assessments are very important to evaluate where you are, how far you have come, and how to proceed from this point on. Self-assessments will give you real data about how your new behaviors and actions are creating changes in your life. It is like pointing to your successful moments. It is also an opportunity to find the areas where you can improve.

Don't use assessments to judge or criticize yourself, that is not the purpose here. The purpose is to manage your life so you can continue making progress and become the person you are designed to be, to be who you want to be. It is no different than checking your bank account and realizing that you need to save an extra hundred dollars each week in order to buy a new car or go on a trip. You are just managing your money. Similarly, self-assessments serve as a way for you to manage your behaviors so they stay congruent with your goals.

How to Do Self-Assessments

There are a couple of ways I like to do self-assessments. One method is done daily. At the end of each day I ask myself, when did I show confidence today (or any other behavior I am working on)? Was there a time that I could have showed more? Remember the first chapter about awareness?

That is what you are doing during assessments—becoming aware of what needs to improve and also celebrating the triumphs. Make sure you are celebrating the successful moments; it won't serve you best if you just focus on the areas where you did not excel. In fact, start with the areas where you did excel, then evaluate the ones that have room for improvement. Our minds naturally tend to be negative, to find what is wrong. You are basically retraining your mind, rewiring your brain to become more positive and look at the weak areas as a place to improve, not as something that is bad or wrong.

You already have everything you need to be successful.

How did you feel when you read the above statement? Did the self-judgment voice appear? That voice appears for me sometimes. It appeared as I was writing this book. I heard, "I suck," "I have no idea what I am doing," and "No one will like it."

Let's get something straight right away: even with a positive attitude and confidence you will still have moments of self-judgment or negative thinking. You are human and you will still have those voices inside you. The major difference between someone who gets how the mind works and has a success mind-set versus someone who doesn't is that they don't attach to those thoughts. You hear that voice but you will not listen to it. You stay on track, committed to your cause and vision. Stay busy doing the things that matter, and you will not hear that voice.

To refresh your memory, in chapter 2, I mentioned that a belief is a thought with emotional energy. My negative thought of "I suck at writing" did not go anywhere, did not stop me from writing, and did not affect my writing at all because I did not put any energy into it. I did not charge the thought. I heard it and ignored it right way. What helps not to attach to a thought is to admit the emotions that come up. Like in my case, I faced the emotion of fear and self-doubt. Once we acknowledge the emotions, we are able to disable their force quickly. It is normal, it is human to fear a challenge, to fear something that we have never done before. We are not here aiming to live a life without any fear—that is a necessary part of being out of our comfort zone. **The highest achievements of your life will never happen inside your comfort zone.** We are here mastering our minds and our life by learning how to move through fear.

A second way to do self-assessments is once a week. Every Sunday grab your journal and review your week. Refer to the same questions as described in the daily assessments. Then make a plan of how you will improve the areas that you found can use a more confident attitude.

The Confidence Killers
1. HARSH SELF-JUDGMENT/LACK OF SELF-LOVE

Do you suffer from "I am not enough" syndrome? The truth is we all have suffered from this syndrome and many still do. This is the core of all issues we face as adults. You may be familiar with the following words that lie below the "I am not enough" statement: insecurity, fear, embarrassment, shame, anxiety, depression, anger, resentment, inadequacy. Here are some of the most common beliefs that you may present or see others presenting:

- I suck at relationships.
- I can't ever make money.
- I can't lose weight.
- I am not pretty enough.
- I don't deserve it.
- I could never get that promotion.
- I am not that smart.
- That is just for rich people.
- I am not worthy.
- That is too good to be true.

You get the idea. We all have stated or at least thought one or more of those sentences. Or you may be saying, not me, I have always been super confident, I don't suffer from this syndrome. Okay, then tell me what area in your life you want to improve and no matter what you do, it never does. I can find the subconscious beliefs that hold the energy of one of those statements. Living with those beliefs can lead to a long life of suffering, from unhappiness to disease and addictions. The emotions of not being good enough have a lot of power and we need to take that power away. We disempower those beliefs by taking actions that empower us and by reframing all those beliefs with new ones that lift us up.

It is very hard for anyone to admit out loud, "I am not _____ enough" (fill in the blank). That is being vulnerable and, for many, a sign of weakness. If that is you, then I highly recommend that you check the work of Dr. Brené Brown. She has done extensive research in the subjects of shame and vulnerability. She says that "being vulnerable is a direct marker of courage." I love that. Think about when you see people being the most authentic, stepping onstage, sharing their stories, and showing emotion. You probably say, "Oh that took courage." They are there feeling super vulnerable opening themselves up. That creates connection, and we feel we are not alone. We all share pain and suffering.

A major problem with this era of technology and social media when everything is shared instantly is that we usually see people happy, in moments of triumph, having dream vacations, marrying the love of their lives, etc. We create this idea that we are the only ones suffering. It is easy to think that life sucks when we think that "everyone else is happy," except, to me, it is an illusion. This 24/7 connection has created deep disconnection. Remember that anytime you see someone celebrating success, that success came with hard work, tears, suffering, and a lot of effort and time to get there. Like writing this book—you may think, "I wish I could write a book, too." Well, *you can*. It took me five years of research; reading an hour or more a day; going to workshops; spending over $20,000 on education; coaching hundreds of people; and having my own struggles with money, a broken heart, and feelings that I am not good enough to get to where I am today.

I am only able to have my dream life today where I write, coach, and do public speaking because of all the effort I put in for years. I tell you right now that many days I was in tears on the floor thinking I would never get here. I had many days where I thought all the hard work was taking me nowhere. This was another illusion. We are always moving forward when we work with purpose and passion.

Stop judging yourself right now. You are an amazing human being who wants to make a difference in this world, who wants to improve yourself because you believe by improving yourself you will improve your life, your family, and our world. You are a badass. I know that about you because you are reading a book about how to master your mind to be extraordinary, to be your own superhero, to be a fit warrior. Welcome to the club of spiritual warriors, this is where you belong.

Now enough talk about how amazing you are. You are asking, "How do I stop judging myself and start loving myself?"

Take the first step and **get out of the victim zone.** I mean it. This is where my tough love comes in. When you picked up this book you made a decision to change your behavior and your beliefs in order to create the life you want. You're in charge. Say this out loud: **I am responsible.** Leave the victim persona behind right now.

You may need a ritual like writing a goodbye letter to that victim inside you. Write and express all your emotions like anger, rage, whatever you need. Say goodbye to that part of you because you are being your authentic self right now: brave, honest, confident, and clear about your direction and goals.

Another ritual that can serve you is to jump in a nice cold lake, ocean, or creek (only if the water is calm, please). Water is so cleansing, it is a great way to wash out the old for the new to emerge. Is it winter? Jump in anyway and scream out loud, "I am a spiritual warrior, and I am ready to live the life I want and deserve!"

Create your own mantra, words that are meaningful to you. These rituals my sound silly, but they aren't. Beliefs are thoughts with emotional charge. You are choosing new thoughts when you go through these rituals. You are charging them with not just emotions but also movement. E-motion is energy in motion. So the act of moving your body when you replace old beliefs with new ones is extremely powerful. Don't underestimate this power. Do it.

You can create any type of e-motion. If you have been to any of Tony Robbins' seminars, you know he makes you jump, scream, and move! This is because you are altering your state of mind by moving. Maybe you want to jump out of an airplane because skydiving is your thing. Maybe you want to climb a high mountain, ski down a steep hill screaming, or go scuba diving. Whatever it is, move with intention. This will create a huge shift in you. Follow up with actions of purpose daily, and your internal world will change. There is no other way.

How to Love the Self

A long time ago, when I was just starting my practice as a holistic lifestyle coach, I had a client in tears, telling me all about her issues and stress. She did not feel she deserved the life she wanted. We talked about self-love and that she needed to learn how to love herself. She asked me directly, "Alex, how do I love myself? What does it look like?" At that moment I realized that I actually had never stopped to define that, so I sat back on my chair and had to think for a minute.

Self-love is a daily practice that involves actions of kindness, respect, and honor toward ourselves. So I responded to her question by saying that she could start loving herself by simply honoring her body every day, eating healthy, exercising gently, spending time with people who enriched her life, and doing things that uplifted her. By doing those things daily, she would be showing love for herself. Self-love begins with intentional actions, then it becomes a feeling. Love is a verb, not just an emotion.

Harsh judgment and disempowering beliefs won't change by simply getting up one day and declaring, I am no longer judging myself or carrying this belief. That is a place to start, no doubt, but that statement needs to be followed by actions of self-love and actions that empower you and charge your new belief. If you have a hard time loving yourself, you will not just change that in one day.

Will you start with the decision to be loving toward yourself from this moment on? Next, you will come up with the actions of purpose that align with loving and honoring yourself daily. Start your 66 days of daily practices and discipline—that is the number of days it takes to establish a new habit—and when you least expect it, you will have this feeling of well-being and peace. And as you work on your self-assessment, you'll realize that you have had many moments of loving yourself, and therefore, you are happier and have more peace. This is success!

2. PERFECTIONISM

This is a big confidence killer. Perfectionism is an epidemic, especially among women, I have found. Our culture, and even women themselves, pressures them to be a perfect wife, a perfect mother, a perfect business leader, a perfect lover. Television, magazines, and the media don't help at all shifting this false belief of being perfect. They show models who look perfect to the eyes of many, but to my eyes they are out of balance and unhealthy. Social media has posts of everyone living a "perfect," happy life. The newscast criticizes the female Olympic athlete who does not smile, but the guys can behave like dumb high school kids and that is okay, it is accepted. The man leaves his wife, and he is supported by his family and friends; the woman leaves her husband, and she hears the criticism, "How could you break up the family?" So ladies, it is hard to escape this false belief called perfectionism, I know.

I want you to not give a f&#k what others will say. That is the truth. You need to stop following the crowd if you want to be successful. Most people choose the easy way, the mediocre way of living. That way means do what everyone else does, be how everyone else is, and believe in what everyone else believes in. Not you, though, I won't let you. You are breaking away from that group. You want more in life, you want to see how far you can go because you can, you want to achieve what others may think is impossible, you want to be extraordinary. Enough of an ordinary life. With that said, you will become an attractor to people who think like you, who resonate with your energy and frequency. You have no reason to fear that you will stand alone. The extraordinary minds will join you.

By the way, what does being perfect mean, anyway? Perfect compared to what? Said by whom? I want you to replace this "perfectionism" word with a much more powerful word: "excellence." Be the best you can be. Be okay saying, "I am not perfect, but I am doing the very best I can." Doesn't that sound much better? Even for the Olympic athlete who trains hours every day for perfectionism, I think "excellence" works better because doing her best means maybe an extra hour of practice every day. Look at Michael Phelps—he decided that for him to achieve excellence and be at his best, he had to swim every single day. It paid off; he has more medals than any other athlete in history. Perfectionism is just a dangerous word because you feel like you are always chasing it but never achieving it.

Do your best, keep working on your potential, and show up. That is perfection.

3. CONSTANT WORRY

Are you a worrier? I used to be one. Worry is fear about the future or the unknown. Worry is a story about something that might go bad. It is bad stress, and it is a waste of time and energy. **Worry is not just a confidence killer, it is a dream killer.** In a state of worry, the focus is directed at the "how": how am I ever going to be able to achieve that goal? Forget the *how* and focus on the *now,* on the present, and just make plans of how you will change your future by the actions you take *today.*

My favorite quote about worry and stress is, **"In the present moment there is no stress."** I can't remember who wrote that. But think of the truth in this sentence. I am not worried about this book's sales, if readers will love it or not, but I hope you do. I am not worried that my English isn't perfect, that the way I write isn't intellectual enough. I am being present with you, writing something that matters to me, and I think it can serve you. I am doing my very best here.

Think of your richest moments with a friend, when you were so present that time stopped and nothing mattered. That is the zone of flow, or zone of genius, a truly creative time. When I speak in public, I get in my zone of genius and the world stops. No stress, no worries, no judgment, no criticism. I am just being present doing what I love.

When you catch yourself worrying, identify the worry. Is it about the future, something totally out of your control? Good, then let it go. If it is something that needs to be addressed right now, take care of it. It is that simple. Does the worry involve someone else? Can you do anything about it? In most cases, no, it is their issue. Relax then, you can only control your attitude, your perceptions, and your behaviors. Don't follow the crowd or the people who are chronically worried, stressed out, and negative. Those emotions are addicting and do not serve you.

A current self-assessment here really helps. The moment you worry, stop and reflect:

- What is it?
- What can I do?
- Focus on an action that moves you forward, that takes you away from that state.
- Don't attach to it if it is just a story in your head. Is it a real worry? Resolve it. If it is not, let it go. Just drop it.

4. UNREALISTIC GOALS

One of the definitions of happiness is, "Results that meet our expectations." If you set excessive or high expectations, your happiness could be highly compromised.

Setting unrealistic goals can be a total confidence buster. It can easily push you into that state of, "I am not good enough." It may give you a great story, such as, "I tried everything and it didn't work." This is a dangerous trap, unless you can recognize early enough that your goals need to be reevaluated and you correct the course of actions.

Set process goals, even daily goals, that move you closer to your final, big goal.

When you set small daily or weekly goals and achieve them all, that pumps up the confidence muscle. Do the opposite and it may atrophy that muscle, costing you a lot of energy to build up again. We are in too much of a rush in this life, but if you are like me, you don't want to waste a minute on activities that don't serve you or take actions that don't matter at all. You want to become a very effective human being and work every day with purpose.

Are your goals realistic? Great, carry on. Not sure? Great, time to reevaluate them. Don't copy anyone else's model, don't compare yourself or your list of actions with someone else's. Comparison is another confidence killer. You need to make a plan that works for you based on time, energy, budget, and logistics. That is building a plan that is realistic for you and that meets you where you are.

As you progress, you may want to make some changes. Set your goals but be flexible about the process.

5. Lack of Skills

This is a tricky one that deserves attention. Skill sets are very necessary to achieve a goal. Lack skills and practice and you go nowhere. Confidence dies in this river of being lost because you don't know what to do.

At the same time, you need to have the wisdom to know how much skill is necessary before you start your endeavor and how much will be learned in the process, as you go. This is why I use the word "tricky."

Many people stop themselves from even starting something because they believe they lack the skills, education, tools, etc.

Take a look at the below list to see if you are ready to start, or if you need to obtain more skills.

- Define what you want to achieve.
- Learn what basic skills you need in order to get started, and practice every day.

- Talk to experts who have done what you want to do; they will share great wisdom that will guide you.
- Hire a coach to help you design a road map.
- Read, take online courses, attend seminars, and continue learning as you go. This is a MUST.
- Get out of your comfort zone and begin.

Test the waters out there. Get started on your adventure once you've mastered some basic skills. Many experts state that it can take ten years to master something. I will add that the only way to become a master is to practice. Make sure you practice the fundamentals over and over and over. Keep it simple. Once you get the fundamentals down, go to the next level, whatever that is for you and your chosen field.

Journal Time

Now that you are clear about what confidence is, take a few deep breaths, become present, and write your answers to these questions in your journal.

- In what areas of your life do you show up with confidence?
- Write down three major moments in your life that showed you had confidence.
- In what area(s) of your life would you like to have more confidence?
- If you bring more confidence to that area, how will that change your life?
- What are the three actions that you are starting today that will build your confidence in that area?
- What skills do you need to acquire or improve to build more confidence in that area?
- Who can you contact that will help you or provide guidance?
- What actions will you take daily to honor yourself?

Write down your manifesto or a sentence about becoming more confident in an area that matters to you. Read it every day and feel it. Close your eyes and take yourself there, to that place where you feel fully confident. Charge those beliefs with your emotions. You always have it all.

Example: From this moment on, I choose to develop confidence in becoming a public speaker because that is my dream. When I am onstage sharing my passion about health, happiness, and success, I step into my zone of genius. I am fulfilled by feeling the energy of the audience.

Four

DRIVE

"Purpose provides activation energy for living."

— *MIHALY CSIKSZENTMIHALYI*

How many times have you been to a seminar and got super motivated to change your life, create a business, lose weight, be more disciplined, write a book, and so on? I bet at least once. Then a few days later, all that motivation goes flat, your enthusiasm dissipates. You flatline. Your mind probably created great excuses for why you should not pursue that new adventure. Common thoughts that occur in times like that might be:

- It is too hard.
- It will take too much time.
- I don't have the money.
- My friends or family won't approve.
- I might fail anyway.
- It involves too many sacrifices.
- I don't have the skills.
- I am too busy.
- It won't make any money.
- It looks like too much stress.

I bet at least one or two of those sentences resonated with you. Maybe they still do if you keep thinking about doing something you really want, but every day you hear one of those negative sentences—the voice of fear, of the ego, of your own shadow. Whatever you want to call it, it is always there.

Maybe this will offer you some comfort: We ALL hear those voices of self-doubt and fear. ALL of us, including the most successful, wealthiest, fit, and famous entrepreneurs deal with this issue. Ask them, read their biographies or stories. They are open about it. They are humans just like you and me. We are all the same in this respect; we all have insecurities and moments of feeling inadequate for a task or a role.

This is why you must activate your superpower, your *drive*. Drive is one of the muscles of your super mind. One of the definitions of the word "drive," according to the Merriam-Webster dictionary, is "to direct the movement of." I will break that down further and say that movement is experience.

Think about how everything we do is movement. Even when you are sitting, your body systems are constantly moving. Your lungs inflate 12 to 15 times a minute; your blood is running through your veins and arteries; neurotransmitters are being produced in your body and brain; essential chemical reactions are happening at the cellular level to keep you breathing, digesting, eliminating, creating, sleeping, thriving, and healthy. Movement is essential for our survival. We stop moving and we die.

Thriving and Desire

Let's get beyond just surviving because we are not living in a jungle. We don't have to watch our back 24/7 because a predator might chase us. We are safe. We have no need to be in survival mode, no need at all. I want you to *thrive*, to operate every day from a place that inspires you, moves you, motivates you, and makes you feel alive.

Look around you and people watch. What do you see? I love watching people when I am out at restaurants or airports. I can see who is just surviving and the ones who are thriving. The ones who are thriving are engaging with someone deeply, they are engaged in their work with enthusiasm, or they are immersed in a book (usually me). I watch their posture, their vitality level, and their energy. You can see that too if you pay attention.

What drives us to move in the right direction? Why is this quality so important for you to live your true potential? There is a root, something big underneath drive that feeds movement and momentum. It is called *desire.*

"Desire" was the name of this chapter initially. But I decided to call it "Drive" because most people resonate with that word more. In addition, to some, desire gives the impression of wanting just power or wealth at any cost. That is not the context here at all. In my vocabulary, the word "desire" means wanting something badly, something that will change not just your life but the life of others as well—the world will benefit from it. You may use the phrase, " I am driven" quite often, but you probably don't use the word "desire" in the context of motivation. I love the word "desire" because the vibration of this word is so strong; it is fire, it is beyond wanting, it is a want attached to a must. Desire feeds drive.

A Weak Foundation

Let's go back to the story of going to a seminar where you filled up your motivation and after few days you felt flat. That is like New Year's resolutions: join a gym, cut out sugar, run four times a week with a buddy, and cook healthy meals. You start off well, the first week goes great. You miss a couple days and then skip a week because of traveling. You get back into the routine, miss a day, go out and cheat on your diet plan, and miss another day at the gym because you are too busy. A month goes by, and you miss the gym for two out of four weeks. After all this frustration, you think, "Forget it, this is too hard, it takes too much time, I can't lose weight, there is something wrong with my thyroid." And the bottom line is you feel bad and ashamed that you failed.

You did not fail on your fitness/weight-loss program. The part that you may have "failed" on was the goals-setting part. Like many, you probably just made a plan and jumped right into it. You skipped a very important part: what and why. You used only enthusiasm, and enthusiasm has a very short shelf life. It deflates quickly, unless you add a "why" to it. So you must ask yourself, **what do you want, and why do you want it?**

Let's recall what adds energy to our dreams and goals: emotions. You need to define what your intrinsic motivation is, not extrinsic. "Just look good in a bikini" is not good enough, it is an extrinsic or external value. You may still want to look good in a bikini, we all do. But beyond that, why? Why is it important to you that you lose weight, look good, and be fit? How will achieving these things change your well-being or change your life? Asking these key questions will help you tap into your emotions and, therefore, energize your emotions, which will fuel your *drive*. These questions get you in touch with the deep, intrinsic values of what you want and why you want it. And the last question is, **how bad do you want it?** What will the consequences be if you don't achieve this goal?

When I talk to clients about their goals and their commitment levels, I get very interesting answers. On a scale of 1 to 10, quite commonly I get a 7. I always want to hear a 10, which means, "I am super committed." When they say their commitment level is a 7, I can be short and playful and just say, "You don't want this bad enough." The reason behind the 7 is fear of failure. I find this fascinating. They are basically telling me, "I am committed, but if I say 10 and I fail, I will be very disappointed."

In other words, they are already sabotaging their goals from the start. They are programming their subconscious mind to work at mediocre levels because failure is expected. Do you remember how our subconscious minds are running the show? That setting below 10 leaves a lot of room to making poor choices that are not aligned with your goal. This is like getting into a relationship with someone and saying that you are about 70 percent committed—we all know how that goes.

Successful people become obsessed with their goals. They commit to a 10-plus; they are determined to do what it takes. They know that the goal will bring them growth, financial success, fulfillment, joy, and more opportunities. They are invested 100 percent.

Change is hard; creating something new is hard. Say you are 90 percent invested. That 10 percent left over will have enough energy and force to sabotage your process. You can't be just 90 percent invested, you must give it your all. That is courage.

Become a 100 percent investor in your goals and dreams.

Your deep and authentic desire to manifest what you want is the foundation of your goals.

You must establish a strong foundation before moving forward because:

- Life will get in the way.
- Some days you will be tired.
- You will have challenges that scare you.
- You will feel like bailing at times.
- You will be judged.
- It is very hard to keep going sometimes.
- You will get disappointed.
- You will have failures.
- You will have self-doubt.
- You will cry.

Desire and your why will get you moving again when those things happen.

Remedies for Disappointment, Downfalls, and Discouragement

Don't panic, don't freeze, and don't run away. There is no lion chasing you. All you are dealing with are your own emotions, and they can be very uncomfortable. Learning how to handle and control your emotions is an essential tool for success. Chapter 5 will cover this topic in depth.

Hear me out: stop and face the challenge and the fear with a warrior attitude. Tell yourself, "Whatever it is, I can handle it." Just by telling yourself that, your stress levels will come down because you are not going into fight or flight mode. You are going directly to a calm state, a mind-set that is solution oriented.

Accept that those emotions that I mentioned above are part of life and part of growth. This is why one of the definitions of stress is "stimulus for growth." It is the upside of stress, the good stress. Stress that comes from working with purpose feeds our soul and brings us a fulfilled life of health, joy, wealth, and great experiences.

You've heard the phrase, "Learn from your mistakes." Perhaps it's a cliché statement, but many people fear mistakes, disappointments, and failure. Embarking on the success path is about embracing all of those things—to be brave, to be bold, to be honest, and to look at those difficult moments with an open and humble heart. Evaluate the setback, understand it, and modify the plan. You just got smarter! That is awesome. When we fail, we learn that there is a better way.

I am a great coach today because of the challenges, mistakes, and setbacks I've had. Without them I would not be able to help people, to write this book, and to live my dream. I needed all those challenges to be where I am. We learn by contrast, by knowing what we want and also what we don't want.

Be friends with stress, failure, and mistakes. Some would say, if you are not failing, you are not succeeding. This is true. What an arrogant attitude it would be if we just moved through life expecting that everything worked out with no challenges and no failures. **The secrets to facing challenges are attitude, energy, and purpose.**

ATTITUDE

"I can handle it" needs to be your mind-set. Ask for help, learn new skills, get a coach, get a mentor, sit in stillness to think with a creative and calm mind. All these actions are fundamental to apply when life gets hard.

If you freeze, just take an immediate action that will remove you from that state of fear. In the state of paralysis your creativity gets killed. In that state there is no flow. In a state of fear, we shut down our intelligence. In a state of fear, we make bad decisions. The new parts of our brain, the pre-frontal cortex where our common sense and decision making live, gets inhibited. That makes sense—if we are running in the jungle to save our life, there is no time to think about what to do. We act from our instincts, from our reptile brain, from our survival mode.

You are not in the jungle, you are just stressed about the loss of money, the mistakes you made, the deadline you missed, the sale you did not make, or a fear of being judged. **Don't make decisions or choices out of a state of fear. That is not your intelligence speaking.**

Attitude is also about your responses to stress, to difficult times. Stress itself is not what makes us sick or kills millions of people every year with heart disease, stroke, and cancer. Our *responses* to stress are what get us in trouble and create more mistakes, errors, sickness, mood disorders, and, in the worst case, death. It is all about how we perceive the stress, the situation, the person. Our perception is what creates internal emotions that can either help us or break us. How do you see challenges? With fear, anger, frustration? Can you look at the situation differently? Having this attitude will save you a lot of aches and pains, plus it will save you energy, a precious resource that we need in order to change and to create.

ENERGY

Energy is your ability to work hard, to endure, to work against force. Energy fuels your power. Energy is your life force. In Chinese medicine energy is referred as our Chi.

> *"Energy is the most fundamental*
> *currency of high performance."*
>
> —JIM LOEHR AND TONY SCHWARTZ

Energy runs our body and our brain. Try doing something with low energy and you know your results will be mediocre. Energy affects every single area in our lives because energy is a holistic concept. I say holistic because one part affects all parts. If you are physically depleted it will affect your work, relationships, health, and responses to stress.

The Holistic Model

We have four sources of energy: physical, emotional, mental, and spiritual. We generate energy constantly from those four resources. Each one is directly connected to the other. For some examples, ask yourself these questions:

- After a crappy day at work, you go home. Does your bad day affect your time with your spouse or family?
- You had a fight with your spouse in the evening. Does that affect your performance at work the next day?
- Your energy is low from not sleeping well. Are you a little more edgy and irritated at work?
- You skipped breakfast because you had an important meeting at work at 9:00 a.m. Are you sharp, fully engaged, and energized?
- You are always tired, so you have no energy for exercise. You get fat. How does that make you feel when you take your shirt off?

As you can see, everything is connected. The whole body-mind connection is real, which is not even a proper statement. There is, in fact, so separation from the body and mind, it is ONE body. But we tend to separate by compartments. We choose to shut down emotions at times in order to get through life. We separate at an intellectual level, so there is this false impression that there is a disconnection between the mind and the body. There is plenty of science now showing us the contrary, however, and it is not woo-woo talk anymore. That means **we are fully responsible for how we feel.** I love this Universal Law.

I love it because that means I have an incredible power to influence how I feel. What a gift that is. Nothing and no one can make me feel a certain way. I can choose.

In a world where many choose to live in a state of victimhood, this is a hard concept to grasp. It is so much easier to say you feel bad because of your children, your spouse nagging you, your workload, politics, the traffic. Or you blame your genetics, your parents, your coworkers.

There is no time or energy for this talk anymore, not if you want to live your best possible life. If you want to see what you are capable of creating in this life, and I will not sugarcoat here, **you need to be responsible for your energy, your attitude, and everything you create,** even the negative experiences. You are always choosing to participate in something, you have a part in it, always! Once you embrace this belief, you take all the power into your hands. The power of choice.

As Brendon Burchard, author of *The Charge,* says, "We don't create energy, we generate it." We can tap into our resources to generate energy all day long. We are designed to have energy all day. The status quo of being tired, depleted all the time, and busy have been accepted as normal in our culture. I don't accept this and neither should you. That is accepting mediocrity. I only accept excellence because that is what we are wired for. **Excellence does not equal perfect, excellence equals doing the best you can with the best there is.**

Energy shows up in our state of presence, not just with one another, but with ourselves and with our tasks and activities. Optimum energy means we show up with full levels of engagement, vitality, and creativity. We are solution oriented, which must be the mind-set of a leader. You are the leader of your life. Lead your life with high energy and excellence, and you will be a great leader to others.

How Do We Generate Energy?
Physical—Movement
Movement is essential for life. Stop moving and we die.

Breath is movement. You can generate tremendous amounts of energy by simply breathing. Breath of fire taught in yoga is an example. It stimulates our life force, our energy, our Chi.

That are numerous ways to move daily. I recommend you move at least 30 minutes every single day. You may choose walking, running, biking, yoga, tai-chi, Qigong, weight lifting, an aerobics class, swimming, dance, etc. Find an activity that you enjoy, that gives you pleasure so you also tap into your mental source of energy. Don't choose something because you "have to"; this may give you energy, but at the same time will create a block in your mental or emotional state that may cause you to leak energy instead. An example of this is when people overtrain and do too much. You may see this in runners, cyclists, triathletes, or CrossFit athletes. They are not creating a balance between energy expenditure and recovery, which is a must for optimal energy, health, and vitality. You can meet someone who works out every day and they don't look vital.

Movement generates energy by activating our biological pumps, deep abdominal muscles, diaphragm, and pelvic floor muscles. Plus, depending on the movement, all the other muscles will also pump blood, oxygen, water, and nutrition to the whole body. This mechanism of pumping is also essential to detox the body by facilitating elimination, which is key for optimal health and energy.

Diet

This topic could cover half of this book. But since this book isn't about diet, fitness, and weight loss, I will summarize it in one sentence:

Food is information, not just a calorie.

The first place to start a great nutrition plan is by cooking whole foods. Eat real food. There is no secret, no magic diet, or one golden book. Shop for fresh foods at your local farmers market; these foods will have the highest nutritional content and life force. Learn how to cook by hiring a chef, taking classes, or getting a book on healthy and simple cooking.

Hydration also fits in here, under diet. Make sure you are drinking plenty of filtered/pure water. You can calculate how much water you need by taking your body weight and dividing it by 2. The result is your water intake in ounces. For example, I weigh 124 pounds, so I drink 62 ounces of water a day.

The foods you choose to eat will give you two outcomes: they will either give you energy or they will rob your energy. If you think your diet is robbing your energy, consult a skilled holistic nutritionist or a holistic lifestyle coach. (Resources can be found at the end of this book, and you can check out my website, www.vitalestudio.com, for my 21-day reset plan.)

Sleep and Recovery

Make it or die, I like to say about sleep. This is the very first place you need to evaluate if you are dealing with an energy crisis, weight gain, or chronic stress. There is no diet, no pill, no coach in the world that will help you with energy until you sleep a minimum of seven hours a night, ideally eight.

We restore our bodies' systems at night. From about 10:00 p.m. to 2:00 a.m. we restore our hormonal systems or most of our bodily functions, and from about 2:00 a.m. to 6:00 a.m. we restore our mental state and refresh the brain. Skip hours of sleep for a few nights in a row, and you will have brain fog, fatigue, mood swings, mental exhaustion, and hormonal imbalance. Skip hours of sleep for weeks or months and you will gain weight, catch colds easily, and become chronically stressed, which is the major contributor to inflammatory diseases.

Recovery and restorative times, besides sleep, refer to time alone for introspection: thinking, meditating, reading, resting, getting a massage, etc. You must have time for yourself to "check in"—check in with how you are, how you feel, and what you need. By doing that you become aware of your state and have the power to make a change if needed. You also become calmer, more present others, and happier.

Physical energy leaks: lack of movement or exercise, poor breathing patterns, too much exercise, poor diet, lack of rest and recovery, poor posture, muscle tension, muscle skeletal injuries, diseases.

Emotional

Emotional energy refers to our relationships, our connection to others, and our connection to ourselves. It also refers to our emotions regarding events from the past like traumas, difficulties during childhood, and heartbreaks. Anything that involves our heart is basically emotional energy; it is heart centered. By choosing connections that fuel our "love tank," or as many say, feed our soul, we generate energy. Think about what happens when you fall in love—you have energy all day and sometimes all night. You feel inspired, motivated, and energized.

Emotional connections are essential for energy and health. When we engage, our brains release pleasure hormones like oxytocin and dopamine. Those are the "feel good" chemicals. Deprive yourself from connecting, and you will get the opposite: no production of those essential neurotransmitters, which will cause depression, low energy, need for isolation, feelings of helplessness, deep sadness, low productivity, and disengagement. Studies show that people who feel lonely and isolated die earlier.

Emotional energy and emotional stress deserve a whole chapter because they are the source of happiness but also the source of the biggest stresses we face in our lifetime. We'll explore more on emotional energy in the next chapter.

Like movement, connections, love, feelings of belonging, and closeness are essential for our existence, for our happiness, and for our success.

Emotional energy leaks: isolation, overworking, lack of intimacy, being around "toxic" people, unhealthy work environment, dysfunctional family dynamics or relationship, excessive time on social media or television.

Mental

Mental energy is generated by our ability to express ourselves and be engaged with tasks that matter to us and relate to our goals. We generate mental energy by engaging in tasks with a purpose and creating projects that have meaning for us because they contribute to our dreams, goals of others we care about, and our life vision.

We need to be intellectually stimulated. When your mental state is stagnated, you are bored. Boredom can be good when you use it as a fuel to think about what you want to create next. It may push you to learn how to paint, play guitar, learn how to dance, hire a trainer for new workouts, go back to school. Boredom can be very healthy, but that becomes not true if you choose to stay in that bored state. Like any feeling of discomfort, it can be good because discomfort charges our needs to change. Stay in that state and you become a victim of your circumstances and life pretty much sucks, all the time. I am sure you have known or know at least one person who lives like that. That is a choice.

Generate mental energy by reading, studying a subject you love, having great conversations, watching documentaries, and learning. Learning is my fuel of choice for mental energy. Second are great conversations. I feel high from rich conversations about topics that I love, like happiness, health, and success.

Mental energy leaks: inability to express yourself, activities or work you don't enjoy, lack of intellectual stimulation, long-term boredom, repressed emotions, poor diet, poor sleep patterns, overwhelm, lack of movement, lack of breaks in the day.

Spiritual

Spiritual energy refers to our purpose, our life's calling, and our connection with a higher power. The higher power may be God, Jesus, Buddha, Muhammad, Ala, Angels, Love, Universe, Source, Higher Self, Spirit, Force—whatever name you give it that resonates with you.

You may say, I don't believe in any of those entities. That is okay, too. You may at least believe that there is an energy in the Universe that connects us all. The energy that exists around us, in the ether. We can't see it, just like we can't see radio waves, but it is here.

I want to talk about the part that you can see and feel—your life's call. Spiritual energy is generated from you living a life that is in alignment with your dreams, your goals, and your purpose. For instance, if your call is to travel around the world and make a living doing it, you create a life that will feed that vision. You learn languages, you save money to go places and connect, you study different cultures, you become an expert in something related to traveling or create a service that others will benefit from and want. You live your life every day connected to your purpose and the Universe will help you. That is spiritual energy.

Many people today come to me for coaching because they are in the midst of a spiritual crisis. That means they don't know what their call is, what they want to do. Or they do know what they want to do but are either too busy to listen or they are afraid of following their call. In some cases, when they have no clue, I encourage them to get curious. Becoming curious generates mental energy that will feed spiritual energy.

Many people don't have the answer for their life's purpose. I didn't for many years. It was uncomfortable! It was not until I became very curious that I found what I wanted to do. That discomfort and curiosity helped me to find the path of holistic lifestyle coaching, and the path of helping people to become the best version of themselves by supporting them through their transformation journey. I found my purpose. The moment l learned what I wanted to pursue, my energy increased immediately. This is the power of mind. Once you see it and believe it, you have it and you own it. You become *it*.

If you don't know your goals, maybe start by simply becoming the best person you can be. Write down what that is, then become that. Define three words of core values. Mine, for instance, are: LOVE, COURAGE, and STRENGTH. I live by those three words. They rule my decisions in life. Start the journey of deep self-knowledge, and with that, I promise, other doors will open for you to explore and find your purpose. After you choose your core values, design your ideal self. Choose how you want to show up. Make a list of the most important qualities to you and become them. That is how you become the best of you.

Spiritual energy leaks: lack of faith in a higher power, disconnection from others, lack of core values and purpose, lack of alignment with your goals and life's vision, insecurities, feelings of not belonging, feelings that you are alone, lack of a community.

PURPOSE

We are all wired to serve, to produce, to work, to expend energy toward things that matter to us. So if we are all wired this way, why are so many people drifting in the sea of life without passion, path, or purpose?

We need a reason to work, to fight. We need the one thing that drives us: LOVE. What do you love so much that is worth fighting for? Purpose is a love, a force that fuels our drive like oxygen fuels fire.

Purpose is our role in this life as creators. What is your gift? What can you offer to yourself, to others, and to our planet? What are you here for? Don't be afraid to ask these big questions. Also, don't force the answers. That can create anger and frustration, the killers of creativity and inspiration.

I want to clarify a myth. You don't need to be Mother Teresa or Einstein or Steve Jobs to feel that your purpose matters. You may think a purpose needs to be something big; it does not. If your purpose is simply to be a great member of your community and help others, being loving and kind to everyone, you've got the greatest purpose, and you are changing the world with your energy of love. Purpose is doing something that fulfills you and serves our world.

Why is purpose so important for a successful life? Because life gets hard sometimes, challenges may take us down temporarily, we feel broken at times from losing someone or being ill. At other times, we may think, what is the point? The point is we have a strong reason to live, to get up, to recover from our hard falls; that reason gets you going no matter what. That is your purpose. You need it. It is the rudder of our boat, it gives us direction, and it keeps us on the right path.

Purpose is bigger than goals. You may have a purpose in your life and not have clear goals. That is okay. A few years ago, I defined my purpose: to live my fullest potential in this life, to live with love, courage, and strength every day. And to help others do the same, to live their dreams. I had no idea how I was going to do that. I didn't know the goals, the plan. I had to create a road map slowly, based on my purpose. Let's say the purpose is our raw draft, our first blueprint, and the goals are the more refined blueprint, with details of what we are creating.

A strong purpose heals any failure scar. This is the word that many fear: failure. Failure will only keep you down if your purpose is not clear, or you don't believe in yourself.

Learn what it takes. Get curious. Explore the world. It is right in front of you. I bet you can find amazing people around you that have walked the path you are pursuing; talk to them. Ask for guidance. Explore your own purpose because it is who you are.

Earlier I mentioned that many people are living in a spiritual crisis, which can manifest as depression and anxiety. Those mood disorders may foster negative emotions such as anger, fear, shame, and overall negativity. Unfortunately, those emotions fuel anxiety or depression, creating a bad cycle.

Finding our true purpose does not need to be hard. It takes inner work. It takes asking yourself the big questions. It takes silence to hear what your mind-soul says. This divine knowledge lives inside you. You just need to open your heart and mind, and it will emerge. **Purpose is spiritual energy.**

The most successful days are the days you are fully engaged with life and with tasks that align with your life purpose and goals. You feel productive, you feel what you did mattered. It is energizing.

In moments when you feel down, weak, somewhat lost—and we all do—keep your eyes on your purpose. Feel it, think it, speak it, embody it. This will remove you from that "funk" that you may face at times. Remember, in times of paralysis and fear, take an immediate action that will move you away from that state. Get moving, go for a walk, get some fresh air, play with your dog. Or simply tell yourself that you matter, that you are in the process of figuring out your purpose or life's vision. You can't give up. The world needs you.

Journal Time

- In what areas of your life can you use more drive and motivation?
- What is your deepest desire right now that will amplify your happiness? Why?
- What are the three latest disappointments, downfalls, or failures you had? Did you deal with them with a growth mind-set?
- If you said no to the last question, how would you change your response next time?
- Is there any area in your life that needs an attitude shift? Why?

Energy Audit

On a scale of 1 to 10, 1 being barely any energy and 10 being tons of energy, evaluate your energy systems.

Mental Energy: ____

- What gives you mental energy?
- What robs your mental energy?

Physical Energy: _____

- What gives you physical energy?
- What robs your physical energy?

Emotional Energy: ____

- What gives you emotional energy?
- What robs your emotional energy?

Spiritual Energy: _____

- What gives you spiritual energy?
- What robs your spiritual energy?

Write down the three new habits you will start now in order to generate more energy.

Do you know your life purpose? If not, do you know your purpose at this phase of your life?

Five

Emotional Fitness

"When dealing with people, remember you are not dealing with creatures of logic, but with creatures of emotion."

— *Dale Carnegie*

Emotional intelligence, emotional competence, emotional excellence, emotional toughness—whatever you want to call it—are all under the expression of being emotionally fit. Being emotionally fit is one of the most important areas of personal development and personal success. In order to handle the stressors of every day, not take things personally, and not let a big setback keep you down, you must develop emotional fitness. Our emotions, when not managed well, can create a tremendous source of chronic stress. Therefore, you must understand what emotional intelligence is to work on your emotional program.

According to the researchers Peter Salovey and John D. Mayer, emotional intelligence is defined as the ability to recognize, manage, and control our own emotions. Today, in my mid-40s, I see the importance of being emotionally fit more than ever. As we get older, we understand more how important relationships are, how much we value those we love, and how the ability to understand our emotions and the emotions of those around us makes us feel more connected to one another. Creating healthy relationships with people we relate to every day is a huge element of fostering happiness in our lives.

Before I dive into emotional fitness, we need to explore emotional stress first. As both a teacher and a student, and over years of coaching clients and observing my own behaviors, I have realized that emotional stress is the one that overloads our minds and bodies the most. It is stress related to the self, how we perceive who we are. Anytime we feel stress that involves others, we are touching our connection centers. Notice how people, in general, are the happiest when they feel connected with others. According to Dr. Gabor Maté, author of *When the Body Says No*, "Human beings as a species did not evolve as solitary creatures but social animals whose survival was contingent on powerful emotional connections with family and tribe."

Our entire lives revolve around relationships, which shape a lot of our beliefs at a very early age. Relationships start with our parents and caretakers. The way parents and caretakers hold an infant, talk to a child, and care for them will program the child's mind. That early brain programming dictates our behaviors and emotions as we grow up. As an adult some of those behaviors don't always serve us. That is why evaluating our relationships can be a great way to evaluate our beliefs about love, friendship, work, leadership, or any other type of relationship.

Relationships to people close to us like our partners, spouses, or best friends can especially be a great mirror of what we feel inside. This is where awareness comes back. For rich relationships we need to be aware of our feelings and the feelings of others. To be emotionally fit, we need to take responsibility and be accountable.

Responsibility

In any relationship, we are 100 percent responsible for our actions and behaviors. We have the power of choice—choice of how we show up and how we react or respond. Being emotionally fit, you never use the phrases, "She made me feel this way," "It is his fault," "I am not the problem, she is," and so on. Remember, this book is about empowering you and showing you how to be your best self, extraordinary, and successful in life. Relationships are a huge part of the success journey; they exist in every single aspect and area of success. How you get along with others, how you are perceived, how you show up, how you connect with people are some of the most fundamental principles of living a happy and healthy life. Therefore, we must be able to be in charge of and master our emotions.

If you are still blaming others for your emotions, actions, and behaviors, I invite you to spend extra time on this chapter and take the time working on your journal at the end. We all place blame at times, we all judge, we all criticize. But when you are emotionally fit, you are aware when you are doing it, and it is easy to correct that behavior instantly. As much as I feel super fit emotionally, I still have moments of judgment in times of emotional stress, but I am very aware when it happens. If I'm in a situation with someone and I feel the adrenaline building up, I try to remove myself from the situation, so I can think with more clarity and analyze what my participation in that conflict is. I take the time to "cool down."

Have you ever noticed that no good comes from two or more people talking when they are upset, stressed, raising their voices, and blaming each other? The egos come up, the voice from the heart gets shut down, and the game of control and self-righteousness rise. No connection ever comes from that place of anger, blame, shame, or resentment. Being emotionally fit does not just give you the wisdom to manage these conflicts better, but also reduces the occurrence of them. I am not sure about you, but I can't stand conflict. I used to avoid it at all costs, to a fault and the cost of ignoring my own needs. It compromised my happiness and well-being. With the help of a coach, I was able to learn how to handle conflicts with grace and love, by simply expressing my own emotions and needs.

We must learn how to stand up for ourselves in times of conflict. This is why it is so important to know our values and beliefs because they guide us during times of disagreement. It is a time to apply our listening skills, so we can have a constructive conversation and not a fight. In times of conflict, some people shut down, some react with tremendous anger. Neither one is a good solution. Both situations build unhealthy stress in the body that can lead to diseases if held onto for long periods of time.

Learning how to communicate without accusations and assumptions is one of the core elements of emotional fitness. In times of conflict, express your feelings and listen, make new agreements with another if needed, and do your best to resolve the conflict. That will give you a great sense of peace. I find one of the best things to do in times that we are challenged by someone is to open our minds, to apply empathy and compassion so we can put ourselves in their shoes. That can bring new insights and information that we maybe were not aware of. Remember that most of time all we want is to be heard and to be seen. More details about this below.

You are responsible for all your actions,
behaviors, and emotions.

Taking Responsibility

So what is my part?, you may ask in times of emotional stress (and I hope you do). That is being an adult, an evolved human being. I will not go into too many details about relationships because it is out of the scope of this book. There are excellent books all about relationships; some are listed under Recommended Reads at the end of this book.

The point here is that you must stand in the fire and not run. In other words, when things get hard with someone you love, your team, coworkers, or friends, you need to ask yourself if you are handling the situation from a place of love, courage, and wisdom. When you speak, are the words helping the situation? Are your words creating connection or disconnection? Are you putting energy toward the solution or the problem? Can you look at the situation differently?

We are 100 percent in charge of ourselves, and in any relationship we play 50 percent of the solution or the problem.

Daily Practices to Become Emotionally Fit
LISTENING

Number one, if you want to feel connected to someone and show up as someone who truly cares and is present, you listen. You don't speak, you listen. You don't interrupt, you listen. You stop the chatter in your head about your own experiences and you listen! **The best communicator of all is the one who listens.**

This is a straightforward concept and still so hard for most people to do. So many conflicts can be avoided if you simply listen, and when there is a pause or the time is right, you say, "I hear you" or "I get you." It can be that simple. Our culture—also my culture in Brazil, not sure about others—have this rude habit of finishing someone else's sentences, or worse, in the middle of a conversation, they start sharing their own story about the same topic and they make it about themselves. Do you know someone like that?

When we listen, we deeply connect with one another. When we listen, we are saying with our energy, I care about you, I care about what you are saying, I am here for you. That is what that person will perceive when you are present and listening. Isn't that amazing? That is what we all want, to be heard, to be seen, and to be understood. You don't need to be an expert in communication, you just need to listen, truly.

Listen to your child, to your friends, to your spouse, or even to a stranger at the coffee shop. We are wired to connect, and to listen is to truly connect.

EMPATHY AND COMPASSION

Empathy and compassion are twin sisters. You can't practice one without the other being there.

Empathy is a true feeling of connection with another person. According to Dr. Brené Brown, "You feel with them, not for them." You can listen, truly listen, without judgment. You put yourself in their shoes so you can feel their pain or sorrow. Don't be afraid to feel their pain. If you can't sit with someone else's pain, it means that you might have a hard time touching your own pain. I encourage you to explore that if this is the case.

Compassion is the feeling that we are all connected by the force of love, or, you may say, God. Whatever it is, we have this infinite energy and force that makes us all one. To look at someone and feel a connection is compassion. It is a deep expression of love.

I used to not be a very compassionate person. It took me heartbreaks, suffering, and inner work for me to learn what compassion and empathy were. Anytime we move away from compassion or empathy, we move away from love, from the essence of who we truly are. We create separation when we judge or blame. We create connection when we express compassion and empathy.

How do we practice compassion and empathy? Slow down to listen and become fully present to feel what the other person might be feeling. If the voice of judgment sneaks in, just take a deep breath and find the love for that person; they might not have the awareness that you have or the same views you do. Love will cancel out that judgmental voice in your head. Being compassionate is a choice. The same way you choose an action, you also choose an emotion. If you practice compassion and empathy long enough, you will naturally become more loving, more present, and more connected to others. Your relationships will be amplified and enhanced.

Vulnerability

"Vulnerability is basically uncertainty, risk, and emotional exposure," Dr. Brown says.

Being vulnerable means choosing to be courageous. It is truly showing the world who we are, letting them see our pain and our shadows, our failures and our strengths, our victories and our successes. It is how we connect best; it is how we connect from our heart. We need to own our stories and who we are. Think of a time when you really connected with a friend. I bet they shared a personal story of struggle, and you felt closer to that person. You felt that your own pain was not unique, that you are not alone.

Another way to look at how vulnerability is a marker of courage is when you see a speaker presenting and you think how much courage it takes to be sharing stories onstage with a big audience. The speaker is being open, vulnerable, even taking risks of being judged or not liked. They are up there anyway. That is courage. I know because I am a speaker and I am always nervous up there, wondering what my audience is thinking. Being vulnerable and courageous does not mean we don't deal with fear of being judged or criticized. We do, we just choose to not let that stop us and define us. Being courageous does not mean not having fear, it means we choose to move through fear. We become vulnerable, we take the risk.

Vulnerability is being true to ourselves and true to others. No matter what the truth is, it is always the path that sets us free. When we create stories that are not our truth, we create a caged life, a life with deep emotional stress that makes us sick in the mind, body, and soul. Freedom is the first step to heal our deep wounds, and the most important step toward freedom is speaking our truth. When we create a gap between our deepest truths and how we appear, we create what I call the "unhappiness gap." The bigger that gap, the more dis-harmony and dis-ease we create. Fear, depression, anxiety, anger, and frustration live inside that gap. Therefore, it is in our best interest to close that gap and to be aware when we are inevitably opening it again. It never disappears, our weaknesses or our shadows will always reopen that gap, but I am giving you many tools in this book to be aware when it is happening so you can immediately take action to close it.

Vulnerability is one of the most important "muscles" we must develop to be emotionally fit. Speak your truth, be yourself. What is the worst that can happen? Judgment? The only ones who judge you are the ones who see your courage and are afraid of their own truth. They will either applaud you or they will judge you. Let the ones who judge you go, you don't want to call them your friends anyway. Your frequency of vibrating love, compassion, truth, and courage don't resonate with them. People come and people go. Be you and you will attract others just like you, it is a Universal Law. **Be bold, be vulnerable, be courageous, be you. Because you are perfect.**

Hacking into your Own Emotions

This book is about success. One of the first steps to life success is to deeply know who you are. It is to understand where you come from, your history, and the history of your parents and even your grandparents. Knowing your history will help you to understand your patterns and behaviors. If we all are the result of programming, our caretakers were the first ones to put "data" into our brains. So we should ask, how did they get their own programs? If a mother is abusive toward her child, she was probably raised around abuse and lack of love. I am not saying it gives her an excuse to mistreat her child, I am saying that everyone carries pain and trauma and acknowledging it leads to compassion and forgiveness—the path for love. Before anybody became our parent, they were someone just like you and me, with fears, doubts, insecurities, or shame. Learn about your parents, especially if you are still holding negative emotions about them. These emotions are hurting you, they are taking energy inside you. You need to let it go.

Being emotionally unstable is the opposite of emotionally fit. You cannot be emotionally fit and hold negative emotions at the same time.

Why do so many people not let go of negative emotions or not deal with them? What is so scary? I still, to this day, find it hard to accept that most people choose to live with masks, create a persona, create unnecessary suffering, instead of facing their deep feelings and emotions so they can be free. It is "easier" for many to live a life of drama and chaos than going deep inside to find out who they are and acknowledge their pain and suffering. You might say, why should I do that and create more suffering? Because that suffering is temporary; it can last a night, a week, a few months, maybe, and then it's gone. The only way to dissolve that suffering is by embracing it because it is part of our story and we need to look at it.

The other choice is to suppress all these emotions and create a lifetime of suffering, and this suffering will be physical, mental, emotional, and spiritual. This is the stress that kills people, the stress that might lead to a heart attack, stroke, cancer, autoimmune diseases, diabetes, and other chronic diseases. We know well now that what creates diseases is only 10 percent genetic and the rest is triggered by our environment and lifestyle. We know this because of the science of epigenesis, which studies our genes and how we can change their function. We also know a lot more about how our thoughts and patterns can change our brain function because of the science of neural plasticity, which shows that we can change our brain wiring and create new neural pathways, new states of brain function. And one of the newest sciences is psychoneuroimmunology, which goes deep into how our thoughts and emotions can change our biology. We can't hide anymore behind the curtain of blame, DNA, or victimhood. We are in charge.

So you can see here that one way to prevent disease is by knowing your emotions. Are they working for you or against you? Not sure? Go back to the first chapter on awareness. Pay attention to your body language—it is relaxed or contracted? When you speak certain words, do you feel good or do you feel a tightness in your chest, stomach, or throat? Your body is talking to you, it is the translator of your conscious and subconscious emotions. All you need to do is start being a witness, that is your journey of self-knowledge.

Another opposite of creating emotional fitness is numbness. When you are numb, you not only block pain and suffering, you also block joy, love, gratitude, health, and happiness. That is the danger. Numbness is not selective. Closing the heart is not partial. You close your heart to avoid suffering, and you close your heart from feeling love, from receiving love, and from authentically giving love.

Whatever the emotional state—trauma, anger, resentment, numbness, or depression—you are not doomed to stay there. Freedom is right in front of you. Love, strength, and courage are inside you, you just need to touch it and use that force to empower yourself. We all have carried pain from our past. Some have gone through terrible traumas but they healed. Some almost died but they healed. Some suffered through poverty and they overcame it. They suffered from deep losses and they found peace with it. If they did, so can you. Stop hiding behind your own story, that you are unique and no one understands you. Stop blaming your parents, your genetics, or the world. Rise now, come out, share your love, share your gifts. Because we need you, the world needs you. It is time.

When you think your pain is bigger or deeper than the pain of others, I call that arrogance. I call that illusion, or just a story in your head. Your pain is yours and you have a unique experience with it, no doubt, but the same things that caused you this pain are shared by others as well. I guarantee it. Don't believe me? Start talking to people, talk to a therapist, a coach, and read books about love, forgiveness, and suffering. You will find many stories just like yours. And that is comforting. You will find strength by being vulnerable with others. You are not being weak by sharing your pain, you are being strong. You won't share a story from a place of being a victim, you will share from a place of being a warrior, of someone who is facing your own shadows, your fears, your dreams, and your commitment of creating a life that you deserve and want.

We live in a culture that for generations has encouraged us to not talk about emotions, suck it up, be tough, just get up and do our job. This is all a bunch of b.s. This is exactly the attitude that has created so much unhappiness, disharmony, disconnection, and disease. Emotions hold energy, they hold a charge that affects every single cell of our bodies. Our cells will be either in a state of growth or in a state of protection. They can't be both.

We are the ones who are going to break this pattern of generations and the only way is to start talking, sharing, and transforming. We are all a byproduct of generations of habits, thoughts and actions. Let's change so we leave a legacy of strength, love, and courage for the future generations. Let's set the tone for the future. I can't change the world by myself, I need you. Please join me. I need your strength, your wisdom, your courage, and your unique talents. No more living in a world controlled by fear, we need love to prevail more. These two forces will always be in play, just like the fables we read and watch, like *The Lord of the Rings*. The force of fear will always be within us, however, it does not have to control us. The more love you allow to shine within, the less force fear will have.

You must master your emotions and learn how to understand them and how to control them if they get charged in a way that does not serve you or serve others. Change the emotions that don't serve you by changing your thoughts and beliefs. That is how you change the subconscious mind, the chief mind that controls your behaviors and emotions. Use the power of your conscious mind by choosing what you want to feel, what you want to experience, what you want to think, and what you want to manifest as your reality. It sounds simple, and it is, but simple is not easy. It takes commitment, desire, deep work, and discipline. But with an open and vulnerable heart; with love and courage; and with the guidance of a life coach, skilled psychologist, energy healer, shaman, or any other practitioner that you trust, this path can be filled with treasures that will lead to a life of freedom, love, joy, and vibrant health. Take the first step, that is how you begin. Be humble, be gentle, and be loving to yourself. And always know that you are not alone.

Journal Time

- Rate your emotional fitness from 1 to 10 (1=not fit at all, 10=very fit).
- How well do you know yourself? In other words, do you understand your actions, behaviors, and habits?
- Do you carry around any emotions like anger, resentment, judgment, and/or fear? Do you know what created those emotions?
- Are you ready to let any of those emotions go and replace them with love, forgiveness, and compassion? Yes? How will you do it?
- How will letting go of those emotions change your life experiences?
- Is it time to work with someone to help you accelerate the process of growth and healing?
- Can you be truthful with yourself and others?
- Are you still blaming anyone in your life for your unhappiness or failures? If so, who?
- Can you find forgiveness, love, and compassion for him or her?
- With the belief that you are responsible for your life, what would you like to change?

Six

"We suffer more in imagination than in reality."

— SENECA

Perhaps the first thought you had when you looked at the word "fearlessness" was that fear is good for us because it can save our lives or keep us out of trouble. You are right. Fear can save your life if you are caught in a dark alley and see someone suspicious who might attack you. Or it may save your life if you see a grizzly bear with her cub on the hiking trail and decide to turn around and run as fast as possible to safety. But how often are you caught in those circumstances? Not often, I hope. That is real fear, needed for the survival of our species. However, our culture lives in fear, or what I call "false fear"—fear that is based on illusion, stories, low self-esteem, self-doubt, limited beliefs, and media sensationalism. Living with a fearlessness mind-set is a must as you navigate the challenges of pursuing the life you want. This attitude is what helps to build courage, to move through difficulties that have the potential to stop you if you give in to fear. You develop an attitude of facing and debunking your own fear, your own illusions. You develop great wisdom distinguishing real fear from false fear.

I know fear; I lived it. When I was growing up in Brazil, I lived in a constant state of fear—fear that gave me anxiety, stress, and took a lot of my joy away. Danger was real there; the city where I lived is dangerous because of the deep levels of poverty and disparity between the rich and the poor. You need to watch your back there, so fear did play a role to help me stay out of trouble.

I understand fear. I feared my dad when my parents got divorced. He did not handle the divorce nicely. I was terrified of my dad when I was only nine years old and it lasted until I became a teenager. Did that fear serve me or save my life? No, because I was not in any danger; my dad just vented his anger about my mom to me and that terrified me. It gave me tremendous anxiety at a very early age.

So is fear always bad? The answer is no, and I will share below when fear is positive, when it is a catalyst for change. However, fear is bad when we fear life, or fear being successful, or fear dreaming big, or fear being ourself, or fear loving deeply. Fear is such a big subject that it deserves its own book.

We have been governed by so much fear that it has contaminated the souls of many people. You may be one of them, and I want to help you transform the energy that is being depleted by fear into energy that you can use for health, happiness, and success. I see way too much energy being wasted in fear that is pure illusion, a lie. I will guide you on this chapter to identify your fears so you can start dissolving them.

There is another side of fear that is positive, and that is when fear is a motivator for change. There is true fear and false fear, and it is fundamental that anytime you face fear, you know the difference, so you'll know how to handle it. I am about to help you find the difference.

Fear can be a great igniter that motivates us to make changes in our lives. One of my biggest fears is to die with regrets, to die knowing that I did not pursue my dreams, that I did not love enough, and that I did not live my potential. This fear got me starting to pay more attention to life, to ask questions regarding what I want, what makes me happy, and what legacy I want to leave behind. I've found the answers motivate me to live big every day, to show up, to live my best.

Maybe you got some bad news about your heart at the doctor's office and changed your diet and started exercising. That is how we transform fear into love—love for life, love for ourselves. We are ruled by two forces in the Universe: fear and love. Taking the fear of being sick and making positive lifestyle changes is choosing love. It is important to note that you want to fuel that motivation by love and not fear. So even though fear was the initial motivator, it helped you to get started in a new path, and love took over. I always encourage love to be the driver because love force is sustainable, fear force is not.

When we operate from fear, we need to rely on willpower, on "I have to" versus "I want to." In addition, when we operate from fear, we turn our senses that we are never safe, that we never have enough money, that we are not loved enough, that we are not healthy enough. It creates a very unhealthy cycle of stress. An example of this is that I used the fear of regret just as an initial catalyst to fuel my desire to live my best life. Once I acknowledged that, I shifted the fuel into motivation by loving life and loving creating the best possible experiences. Love is the fuel.

Living A Fearless Life

Now that I have clarified that not all fears are bad, I will move forward in detail about the fear that *is* bad for you—the false fear, the one that paralyzes you and holds you back from living a life filled with joy. Living a fearless life does not mean having no fear. It just means that you will move *through* fear because your dream, your love is bigger than the fear. We cannot get rid of fear, but we can learn how to dance with it, look fear in its face, and use it as a motivator or a teacher. So fearless is simply choosing not to focus on fear, not to let it define you and your actions. **Fearless living is an attitude, a powerful mental muscle.**

Fear comes dressed in many ways. It shows up as anger, frustration, perfectionism, rage, anxiety, depression, and disease. Fear is a pure form of emotional stress. Most of the stress people face today is related to fear. Fear of not having money, fear of a broken heart, fear of losing a job, fear of not being accepted. These fears are created in our minds, based on stories we tell ourselves. Are the stories you tell yourself real? As far as the mind works, yes, the stories are always real. The mind does not know the difference between what is real and what is not real. That is a powerful ability we all have because it generates our manifestations—it all begins with a full concept in our minds. But like any power, you can use it toward the light or toward the darkness.

Back to the story of my dad, I thought he was dangerous, even though my mom always said he was not. That fear felt real to me, therefore my biology responded with anxiety. He was not dangerous, but the thoughts that he was dangerous caused me mood problems. This is an example of how it is not the stressor that changes our physiology, it is our response to the stress that does.

You know how false fear can manifest in someone's life? There are tons of examples of how people fear something so bad that they manifest it, like disease. We live in an era where we fear so much. We fear cancer, we fear the water we drink may be poisoned, we fear the effect of GMOs in our food, we fear the meat we eat might be contaminated, we fear shootings at schools, we fear terrorism, we fear deadly contagious viruses, we fear death. I am not saying all these issues are not real—quite the opposite, they are very real. But it is also real that the world is safer than it used to be, according to research. We live longer, we cure diseases that used to kill us, we have access to healthier choices, and the chances that we will die from a terrorist attack are very, very small. So what benefits will you have by living with the fears in your head? None. There are things that we absolutely have no control over. It is a waste of our energy resources to put any thought into those subjects. Unless the threat becomes real and it is really happening in front of us, it is just a story. Don't let a story rule your life. Or if you do, then choose a story that is life and dream affirmative. What I mean by that is, if you fear so much that everything may end tomorrow or next year because of a prophecy or an intuition, then start living now. There are two types of people: those who freeze with fear and those who use fear to fuel life. I want you to live, to laugh, to take risks, to pursue your dreams, and to love without worrying about a broken heart.

When you think of the best moments of your life, did they come with fear? I bet the answer is yes! You started a new relationship, you got married, you started a business or a new job, you made an investment that worked out great, you jumped out of an airplane, you moved to a new country, and so on. You chose to be courageous. Courage is not the opposite of fear, by the way; courage is the action of moving through fear.

The "opposite of fear is joy," says Dr. Lissa Rankin in her brilliant book *The Fear Cure*. To reinforce the statement that joy is on the other side of the fear coin, I will use a paragraph from the book *Courage* by Debbie Ford:

Every time we make a choice that is based on fear, we are sealing in the belief that we are unworthy, that we are not good enough or not strong enough to be in control of our own lives, our thoughts, our beliefs, our choices—and, most important, our future. Every time we make a choice based in fear, we teach our minds to believe that we are helpless, hopeless, and powerless—three emotional states that leaves us feeling like a victim.

The opposite of joy is really living with those emotional states that Ford describes. I see that up close, every day when I coach clients. They fear not having money when they have plenty in the back account. They fear loneliness even though there are plenty of people who love them. Choices based on false fear give us the sense that we are never safe, the sense that we never have enough, and that creates a cycle of constantly seeking security, safety, and love outside ourselves. This is a search filled with disappointment because we can't find those things externally, we all carry them inside us. The false fear says you need to search out, love says your search is within. Ford says, "We need to become warriors of love," and I completely agree with that. We need to act from our deepest strength, power, and integrity. We need courage to weaken our fear, we need courage to access our true power.

How we Develop More Courage

Courage is like a muscle; we all have it, but it is stronger in some of us because we use it. You have so much courage in you, sitting there in your body, ready to be accessed 24/7.

Think right now about all the main events from your past that required you to face fear and you went for it. Dig in, go deep, I am sure you can find a few events back in your memory, even if you go back to childhood.

Here's the deal: you are reading this book because you are interested in personal growth, and you are wondering how you can up level yourself, take your happiness factor to the next level, and embrace the successful person that you are. That takes courage. The opposite of that is to do nothing, to deny growth, to avoid challenges. That is not you, you are courageous.

The very first step to strengthen our courage is to get to know ourselves, learn about our gifts, our strengths, our talents, and how we can serve this world. We tap deeper, we find our wounds, our fear, our pain, and we face them so we can heal, that is courage. To look at the center of our own hearts and admit when we are wrong, or when we can do better and then we do better, that is courage. To look someone in the eyes and say, "I love you," to hug a stranger, to speak our truth, to be ourselves, that is courage.

So how do we strengthen this superpower every day? **We practice vulnerability every day. We show up in authenticity without apologies. We define what matters to us, what core values we hold in our hearts, and stand for them.** Think of these actions like the weight-lifting program for your courage muscle. You have to do the work if you want to get fit, and you've got to do the heavy lifting to keep building strength and stamina.

What risk have you been holding back from taking? Have you been wanting to quit your job to start your own business? Do you want to leave a relationship that is not serving your highest good? Do you want to open your heart to love? Do you want to travel to Europe alone? Do you want to learn how to play the drums? Go for it! What are you waiting for? Is the fear voice speaking to you, saying, why do it? Does that voice sound something like, "You are fine just doing your thing every day, who do you think you are, you are too old for this, you have children to care for, you don't have the money." That voice will always be there; it is up to you to listen to it or not.

Courage says don't listen. The courage voice from your heart, from your soul, says do it all. If that dream will bring you experiences that feel fulfilling to you, then jump, dive into it. Don't worry about how you are going to do it, just take the first step, and the Universe will guide you for the rest of the journey. If you want to know all the details of how, what the outcome will be, and need to wait for the perfect moment, you may never do it. Because the perfect moment is when your heart is ready. The perfect moment is when your love for the idea or for the vision is bigger than anything else. The perfect moment is now. Close your eyes and imagine your life as if you have that already, as if you are living that dream. How does it feel? What emotions are running through your body when you feel that dream manifested? Your body tells you how much you want that. If your body says yes, now is the perfect time.

Here is my take on changing your life to pursue a dream and to take the risk that may cost you: Can you live with the idea that you took the risk, learned a lot, and it did not work? Or can you live with the idea that time went by, you got older, and you never tried because of fear? Which one is it going to be?

When I opened my own business in Boulder, Colorado, those two questions were crucial to my decision. Do you know what happens in this economy when you want to open a business that costs $3700 a month just in rent, plus all the other expenses? Many people said it was risky and that most small businesses fail in the first two to three years. The odds play against us in moments of big decisions like that. And even with all those "scary" facts, I knew in my heart that I wanted to open that business. I made peace with the fact that it could fail and I jumped. I could not live with the idea of letting life pass me by thinking, "I should have done it." A study was conducted on what people near death regretted the most, and most of them said they regretted the things they never did, they never regretted the things they did. We all can get over losses and failures, but to end up late in life imagining all the things that we could have done and did not do because of fear would be the most ultimate failure that could not be repaired.

I am all for a world of positive psychology bombarding us with "think positive" mantras, but we also need to be truly realistic and look at the side of what can go wrong. We need to think positive, but we also need to look at the negatives and prepare for them. That takes courage. If my business failed today, I know I would be okay. I would be okay waiting tables again if I needed to, I would be okay doing odd jobs for a while to get myself back up again. I took a calculated risk, but I also had faith, trust in myself, and trust in my ability to handle difficulties that might arise.

So fear, this is what I have to say to you: I hear you, I acknowledge you, I know my risks, I know my sacrifices, I know how much work it will take, and I say YES to myself, I say YES to my dream because I am worthy, and I am capable of figuring things out and getting through the challenges.

Which is it for you? Are you ready to say yes to life? What do you have to say to your fear?

The Biggest Fear

I might know the type of fear that is holding you back—one is called unknown and the other is called uncertainty.

Most people will not make changes in their lives, even though they are unhappy, because of control. Unhappy, unhealthy, and dysfunctional are known ways of being for them. To change into a new way of living, being, and doing is unknown. That is scary for many, but it is my hope that with this mental fitness guide I am sharing with you that you transform that fear into excitement.

Let me debunk something for you right now. Fear of the unknown is fear of an illusion. It is a lie. To believe that you know what tomorrow will look like for sure is an illusion. The only certainties in life are that life is always changing and that someday we will die. This is not a pessimistic view, it is a realistic view. It is way more fun to embrace the changes and go with them, growing and learning in the process, than to resist the changes. There is no guarantee of anything. Many people know this but only on an intellectual level.

Sometimes we need a big wake-up call to make us realize that nothing stays the same and to see how fragile life can be. For me, that call was the 9/11 event. Seeing those two towers being destroyed by an act of human terrorism, an act done intentionally to destroy lives, was my wake-up call. Imagine you go to work one day, you are grabbing your coffee, chatting with your coworker, and in one second, that all changes. Can you prepare for that? Never.

We have had so many examples of random violence in the last few years. School shootings, movie theater shootings, the bombing at the Boston marathon, racial encounters with police that ended up in deaths, and the list goes on. We need to wake up. We need to realize that life is precious, life is short, and we have only this time here, in this physical world, to have great experiences. Great experiences are not all happy, joyful experiences. These are meaningful experiences and that will come with joy and tears, with playfulness and pain, with victories and losses.

All experiences that come to us come to teach us, to help us grow, to help us evolve. We always have the choice to embrace the pain, embrace the challenge, or resist. I encourage you to embrace it, to listen to the pain, to look at the challenge with the eyes and mind-set of pure potential and possibilities. This is the secret mind-set to deal with changes, transitions, and challenges. You can focus on how terrible the change is because there is loss involved, or you can choose to focus on the potential for something amazing to come—because there is always potential. Potential is a neutral place, it helps us to move from a negative state to a neutral state, since jumping right into a positive state might not feel authentic. The mind-set of potential and possibilities have an incredible power to create a bit of relief in times of pain and suffering.

The Difference Between Pain and Suffering

Most people might believe that pain and suffering mean the same thing. In my own experience, my own spiritual journey, I have found there is a difference. This epiphany came to me after a great friend who is a spiritual coach shared with me that we don't need to suffer. This is someone who was going through an extremely tough time in her life. When she said that, I stopped and said, "Don't we need to suffer to learn, sit on that suffering, and deal with it in order to heal?" She said, "No, we can feel the pain, but we don't need to suffer." After that conversation and after doing some research on fear, I came up with my own conclusion of what the difference is.

Pain is the emotion of sadness, grief, loss, and despair. We accept the change, the loss (such as finding a new life after a divorce, grieving the loss of someone we love, losing our job, or losing a pet), the transformation, the transition time, which can be very uncomfortable. Loss will create difficult emotions that will give the sense of suffering. Pain and suffering walk side by side. We will suffer if we resist the change or the situation. That is the line between pain and suffering: acceptance.

Imagine your wife asks for a divorce because she is not happy, she needs to expand her soul development by being alone, or she fell in love with someone else. This might cause great pain, deep sadness, and disappointment. This might cause a temporary depression, a sense of being lost and helpless. But when you accept it, you accept that your partner needs to follow her heart, that maybe that soul contract with you is over, that it simply means the love for you will take a different form and can still be as deep. You accept the new circumstances, and as hard as they are, you just accept what you cannot change. If you resist it with fear, anger, or resentment, you are creating deep and lasting suffering for all the parties involved. **Pain is temporary, suffering can last a lifetime.** You can create long-term suffering for yourself by attaching your thoughts to a story—the story that marriage is forever, that divorce is wrong, or that you will never love again. **What creates the suffering is really the attachment to a belief.** If you let the belief transform into a new one that creates acceptance, love, kindness, and compassion, you will dissolve that suffering in a minute, in a week, in a month. It all depends on your emotional state and in your commitment to transformation. You don't have to do years of therapy to transform the suffering into temporary pain, pain that, if faced and embraced with love and compassion, passes. It always does.

Pain is an invitation to transform and to grow. Suffering is the belief that you have no choice. This is another big lie. You always have a choice. Is there anyone in your life whom you are holding in a space of suffering? If yes, can you open your mind to accept the situation? Can you look at the person or challenge with different eyes? Can you look at the pain as a teacher? Is there an area where you need to learn acceptance?

Acceptance brings immediate peace. Even when you are hurting, it soothes the wound. It is amazing to feel peace in your heart when you are sad, in grief. That peace allows you to feel, to get in touch with your emotions, and sit with them. It is okay to feel sad, to even be angry for a while. Allow yourself to feel the pain; it is absolutely necessary for our own process of healing and growth. This is how we can move on and create new, amazing experiences. Acceptance is one of the most fundamental aspects of living a happy life.

We are living in an era when most people don't want to feel pain. They medicate with alcohol, drugs, sex, and other distractions like social media. People go to doctors and ask for antidepressant medication when truly what they need is to sit with the pain of sadness. They are sad, they are feeling down because of the loss of someone or the loss of a story they had for their lives. We cannot medicate to avoid that process. That energy created by the pain needs to be dealt with; you can't just hide it or suppress it. When you do that, that pain will get manifested in your life in the form of physical disease or emotional stress. It will show up in your intimate relationships, in your relationships with people you love, it will hold you back from being your best self. That pain that is not dealt with will carry energy that will always affect you in negative ways. It is like carrying a bag with you on a trip with filled with a bunch of rocks—you don't need them, but you are carrying them anyway, and they will slow you down and give you back pain, blisters, and unnecessary discomfort. Drop that heavy pack now by simply changing your story. Drop those rocks!

Why do we Fear Pain so Much?

We fear pain because looking at our pain involves us getting really real, becoming truthful with ourselves, becoming vulnerable. That pain may bring shame and guilt. With that approach, I can see why most people don't want to look at or feel their pain.

Can you do that process with love and compassion instead of shame and guilt? That is what cultivates courage and wisdom. Owning our pain, our role, our responsibility in any situation is one of the most courageous acts. To stand up when we hurt and say that we are part of that story, that we created those circumstances, is brave. To blame and judge is not courageous, this is being a victim. It is being childish, like a little girl or boy having a tantrum. Anytime we play the role of the victim, we are acting like a child, thinking that we have no choices, no power, and we were abused or taken advantage of. No one can do anything to us without our permission.[2] No one can steal our minds or our souls.

Get Underneath Fear

I have been sharing with you definitions and insights about fear, but now you may be asking, "How do I face fear?" There are many ways, and what I am about to share is based on my own journey and what I have learned from spiritual practices and spiritual teachers.

---

2 I am not referring here to victims of physical or sexual abuse.

Start by looking at the stress in your life. Name the "nightmare," the one thing that keeps you awake at 2:00 a.m., that makes your body contract, that brings with it other faces of fear, like anxiety, depression, mood swings, anger, resentment, or overwhelm. The nightmare is that stress that if you were to eliminate it, it would bring more peace into your life. It would give you a feeling of freedom.

Once you name the stress or nightmare, get deeper, get underneath that stress.

What is it? How did it get this bad? Why is it affecting your life? Dissect that stress/fear. It is real? Is it false? Is it something you can change, or is it time to accept it? Are you blaming someone? Are you ready to take responsibility for your part? Are you ready to let it go?

Let's play a scenario so you can understand this process better. I will share my thoughts (in italics) as it unfolds.

A client came to see me to help her with stress at work. She shared with me that she was not feeling safe at work, that she always felt anxious, and she was afraid that she could be let go anytime. She was feeling instability in her job. She started feeling that way after seeing a coworker, who was also a friend, be fired.

I asked her what her fear of being fired was based on, and she responded that it was based on her friend's experience. *I inquired here about the root of the fear so I could see if that fear was real or false. I determined she had a history of anxiety.*

I dug a little deeper and asked her why she had not approached her boss yet to express her concerns. She said that her friend had done that and she was not well received. My client felt that there was lack of transparency at work. *You can see here that my client's fear was coming from a story of her friend. She did not know both sides of the story, only her friend's side. We don't know here what really went on between that friend and the boss.*

I encouraged my client to face her boss and share her concerns. She seemed worried about doing that, but at the same time, she thought it was the right thing to do. She had a lot of fear around that.

At that point I did an exercise with her where she had to write down the triggers of the fear, the beliefs behind that fear, and the symptoms of that fear. I then asked her to write down occasions when she felt safe, when she felt stable in her job, and when she felt she was cared for.

Next, I turned the perception of this fear around on her. I asked her if she truly wanted this job, if she really wanted to be there. Second, I asked if maybe she was feeling unstable in her life and maybe unclear of her life's goals. *These questions are very helpful to turn a situation around, especially when you blame others for your negative emotions and stress. This is a way for you to take charge of the situation and see what the root of that fear is.*

She expressed that she was not sure about her life's vision and goals and that was somewhat stressful for her. She also expressed that she was becoming careless at work, less engaged. *This is where I saw a subconscious sabotage because if she kept being careless, she would manifest her biggest fear—being fired.*

My final advice in this session was to encourage my client to become very clear if she really wanted that job. That maybe the fear had nothing to do with the work environment and more to do with her fear of creating a career change.

This is a great example for two growth lessons:

1. What we see as a stressor isn't the real stress. Our egos jump into blaming others for our discomfort when our discomfort is really a call from our soul to create a change. It is a call for us to look inside for answers and guidance.
2. Fear is a teacher, a guide. As Dr. Rankin writes in *The Fear Cure,* "While fear can be a vehicle for growth, shifting your beliefs so you feel less fear only makes your transformation easier. We have to be careful about the beliefs we put into our minds about our relationship to life's stressors and the fears that can accompany them."

If we embrace fear and stress as guidance systems, we can make decisions based on our truth and not on false fears. Using fear as a guidance system invites us to look at places that need healing or to look at beliefs that are not serving us anymore. You don't want to get rid of fear or just ignore it, ever—that will just make fear gain more force and on a subconscious level will hold you back from taking steps toward success and a fulfilled life. To ignore fear is to ignore some truth inside that is trying to get your attention—a place for growth or a place for healing and transformation. Avoiding the truth can make you lose years of having a life that you love, a career that feels like a calling, and a healthy body that feels energized every day.

I want to remind you that every kind of stress—physical, mental, emotional, and spiritual—appears to get your attention. Listen to that stress, that voice of fear, with love, compassion, and an open mind. It can be scary because it might me a voice asking for change and change is hard. However, change cultivates courage, change takes you to a life that enriches you and those around you.

Anytime you are living a life that is not in alignment with your deep desires or your soul's calling, the Universe will send you messages. These messages could be telling you that is time to stop, create stillness, and search for your inner truth. They can be as gentle as just seeing consecutive numbers, like 111, 222, 333 over and over on license plates, clocks, or sales receipts. These messages can also be harsh, like losing someone or losing your job. If you trust that everything is always happening to expand your soul and amplify your life's experiences, you will navigate through rough waters with courage, integrity, and strength. You will go with the flow instead of resisting that natural course of life. If you resist the inevitable changes of life, you create suffering, suffering that can last years, or even a lifetime. I see people in their 80s and 90s who still operate at the emotional and spiritual level of a child. They grow old with anger, resentment, and bitterness. That to me is a tragedy, an abuse to the body, mind, and soul, a life wasted with fear.

I am here sharing this book with you because I don't want that to be you. I am your coach right now, your teacher, your cheerleader because I want to make a difference, I want to create a happier, more loving, and healthier world, and I need you. When you live your truth, you are authentic, you love, you take great care of your health, and you create a community where you won't hurt others and you won't hurt our planet. Those committing violence against each other, against animals, or against our planet are living in deep fear constantly, they are letting fear rule their lives, and they disrupt harmony, balance, and peace. I want to build an army of love warriors, of courageous warriors. Be part of my army. Let's spread love, compassion, health, and happiness together, because together we are much stronger. Make friends with fear.

Journal Time

- If fear did not exist, what would you do? What changes would you make in your life?
- Write down three occasions in your life when you faced your fear and won. Or if you failed, what great lessons were learned that made you stronger?
- You know your fear. It is true? Does that fear hold truth? What is the worst case scenario if you move forward through the fear?
- If you can't move through the fear and make a change or shift in your life, what consequences will that bring in your life?
- Your fear, is it yours? Or does it belong to your mom, dad, or someone close to you?

Seven

*"NEVER give up on something that you can't
go a day without thinking about."*

— *UNKNOWN*

Grit is endurance, the ability to sustain drive, and perseverance toward our goals or dreams. Angela Duckworth, author of *Grit: The Power of Passion and Perseverance* says that "grit is a predictor of success." In her own words from her TED Talk she describes how "grit is passion and perseverance for very long-term goals. Grit is having stamina, it is sticking with your future day in and day out. Not just for the month, [but] for years. Grit is a marathon, not a sprint."

Grit is another mental muscle that is necessary for you to work daily in order to get stronger and increase stamina. In other words, without grit, the journey to success can be grueling if not impossible.

Impossible is a strong word, but the journey to success involves sticking with our goals, still believing in our dream when things fall apart—and things do fall apart sometimes. Grit is the muscle that will get you up when you fall.

Grit is what leads us to self-mastery. Grit is what gets us moving in times that we want to give up, those times that we are so close to our goal and we don't see it, but we keep going. We just don't give up.

Grit must be accompanied by passion, though. This is how you know when it is time to quit something because after a while you find that the passion is not really there. It happens and that is okay. How many times have you tried something or started a new path with excitement, and a few weeks or months later you dropped out? My hand is raised, I done this many times. I tried theater, martial arts, guitar, piano, archery, and even tried a new career, firefighting. After all the grueling training, I decided it was not for me.

In fact, one of my places of shame used to be just that—not finishing things I had started. My mom made sure to remind me of that when I moved to the United States. She was not happy; she mentioned that I was just like my dad, who never finished things and changed his mind a lot. She was right. I was not sure what my passion was in my teens and early 20s. I was lost, but I knew one thing: I was living a life that was not right for me. A life that felt off, that felt it did not belong to me. I was in the wrong place, I thought, in my 20s. Then, through spiritual growth I realized it was just perfect. Nothing is ever wrong in our life. I was exactly where I was supposed to be, in Brazil. Even though I did not like my life, it was the perfect place, the perfect life, which gave me reasons to seek something else. I was bored in Brazil and boredom can be the greatest state to ignite creativity and change.

Passion is the spark of grit; passion is the fuel that motivates us. However, passion alone does not guarantee any success. If you just use passion, it is like a honeymoon phase, romantic and magical, until hard times come, and we all know they do. After your honeymoon phase, either in your relationship or in the pursuit of your fitness, financial success, or any goal, what will sustain the process is grit.

What if You are not Sure this Path is your Passion?

Here's the deal: you won't know completely if the path you are on is your true passion until you immerse yourself in everything that is involved within your vision, goal, or dream. The following story will illustrate this point.

In 2003, I hit my first career crisis. After the second one hit, I ended up finding this path today, which I LOVE. I had decided that first time that I wanted to become a firefighter. There is the superhero aspect, it is dynamic, it pays well, I would be able to work out a lot, it had great benefits, and it fit my badass personality perfectly. So I started my journey. I gathered some info about where to apply for the jobs here in Colorado. It was tough, there were not many paid departments around here. A lot of the fire departments are all volunteered based, except the higher positions. But I wanted it so bad that I did not care, I could start as a volunteer if I had to. I had passion and grit, no problem.

I did not get recruited to work in any paid department—my scores on the written tests were not good enough (I have never been great on multiple choice tests) and there were very few positions in the state.

I became an EMT (emergency medical technician) and ended up getting accepted at the Mountain View Fire Department, a few miles east of Boulder. I showed up for the first intro before training started. I walked into the classroom and I was the only woman. There were 26 men and me—a small girl weighing 125 pounds with an accent. I thought, I will be crushed here. Most of the guys were 225 pounds or more. (There is a point to mentioning the weight, I will get it to later.)

Training lasted the whole spring. We all got our bunker gear, a partner, badges, and a mean lieutenant who looked like a pissed-off marine. He loved to yell at us. Then there was this guy from the Bronx with a heavy New York accent. He was a giant and was one of our trainers.

Training began and I realized right away that I had a huge advantage over 90 percent of the guys. I was fit, fierce, and I had grit in me. We had drills that required a lot of endurance and effort, and we had to wear this heavy gear in 85-degree weather some days. For anyone who was not healthy and fit, they got toasted.

Weeks went by and the mean lieutenant was leading us through a rescue drill in a building. We had to learn how to crawl through windows on fire, find a body, and drag the body out of the building though the window. No fire, just a simulation. My turn came, adrenaline was rushing,

I thought, "I can't mess this up, I hate being yelled at." I got the body and I dragged a 250-pound guy like I was a superwoman. The lieutenant says to all the guys, "This is how it is done." I was so proud. In that crowd, as a woman, I had to prove myself that I could handle the job. I gained respect from everyone.

Graduation day came, and the big trainer from the Bronx came up to me and said, "Brazil"—that is what he called me—"I will go into the fire with you any day." I still get goose bumps just remembering this.

In the firefighting world you are always assigned a partner, the person who will watch your back, who will save your life. For him to say that to me was the best graduation present ever. Training was brutal and I finished at the top of the class.

I worked two shifts at the firehouse, and I quit.

What happened? I did not lose my grit, I discovered that, after all, I was not passionate about the fire service at all. When I sat around the firehouse waiting for calls, I realized how much I missed being active, talking to people, teaching, and stimulating my brain socially and intellectually.

I loved the training and I had created a fantasy about the job. But I could not see myself in that career path. So, I went back to being a fitness trainer.

Some may ask, should I have stayed longer to maybe redevelop my passion? Not in that case. I was flat, there was not one ounce of desire in me to stay. I experienced what I needed.

Do you call this failure? Some might. I don't see that as a failure at all. I don't see failure in experiences that teach us so much about ourselves. The life lessons I learned, the confidence I gained, and the grit I saw I had were invaluable tools that got sharpened through that journey. There was no money, time, or energy wasted. It was an incredible investment in myself. Plus, having that "detour" in my career gave me more appreciation for my work as a personal trainer. I got more education and became one of the best professionals in my field.

Follow your Heart

I doubted this statement for a short time. It was around the time that I hit my second career crisis in 2010 to 2011. The passion light was dimmed. I felt my work had gotten flat, like stagnant water. I was not seeing the results in my clients, I was in worry land, I was not my best, and I was not present. I was having a major identity crisis. I was one of the best trainers and I was always struggling with money, making the same amount every year, having ups and downs. I was so tired of the struggle. I began questioning the "follow your heart" motto, which was starting to seem like a bunch of crap. I was ashamed of being 40 years old and not having a decent savings account or enough money to travel, worrying about how much dinner with friends was going to cost. I got angry, and anger can be good when you can channel it toward change. I had hit my *enough* time.

The hard part of this crisis was that I had no idea what I wanted to do next. I was a bit lost. As a personal trainer, you don't have a career path, really. You either manage a health club or open your own business—two things I did not wish to do at that time.

So, I started exploring my options. I loved food, coffee, and people. I loved hanging out in coffee shops, and I always complained that I could not find healthy food to go with my espresso. Brilliant. I decided I wanted to open a coffee shop with organic foods and great healthy sandwiches and salads. I believed that I was going to open the best coffee shop in Boulder.

Well, I did not open a coffee shop. When I started picturing myself waking up at 4:00 a.m. every day to prepare foods and open the shop, I realized that I did not really want to do it. It was about this time that I came across a book called *Force of Nature* by Laird Hamilton. In that book, he talks about Paul Chek being his coach. Remember that Paul Chek was my teacher? In that moment when I saw Paul's picture, I knew my new path. My pursuit to become a holistic lifestyle coach began. All the pressure of figuring out my life's path was gone. That crisis was resolved.

A Bit More about Me

Let me back up a little. Something about me is that I always want to be the best I can be. When I moved to the United States, my first job was at Pizza Hut as a cook. I did not know any English and I needed money. The $2000 that I had when I came here was gone in a few weeks. The only way I could stay in the country was if I found a job. A day after I cried hard because I would have to go back to Brazil, I got a job at Pizza Hut. I was so happy. I cooked many deep-dish pizzas there at the La Jolla store in San Diego. I was so good that the manager approached me to see if I wanted to pursue a career at the company because I could manage stores. I felt flattered but said no thanks. I quit and got a job as a server in a sushi bar. That was a promotion in my world.

This is an example of how a long-term goal carries us through during times that we need to do whatever it takes to keep moving forward. I was not passionate about cooking pizza, but I was in love with the idea of making a life in the United States. I did not care if I had to wash dishes and clean the floors, I did all that. I was happy. I was following my heart.

Follow your heart always, but have a plan and be willing to do work that is not always fun. Find people who can support you along the way. Find a mentor, a teacher, a coach, or at least a friend who can be your cheerleader.

I realized just a few months ago the reason I love being a coach. I love people's stories and their journeys to success, but I have found there is another, deeper reason I love my work. I have become the coach I wish I had when I started college. I had so many challenges, and I did not have anyone who I thought could really help me. I became the person I wish I had when I was lost. I found in myself what I was missing in life. It was a very cool moment for me to understand this archetype of a teacher, a mentor, and a warrior. I know where it all came from. That is why I say I was born in the right place. Brazil taught me many beautiful lessons that I needed in order to be able to teach what I teach today.

I can say with full confidence that I can coach people from a very authentic place.

I know pain, I know courage, I know love, I know fear. I suffered during heartbreaks. I was scared many times. I was weak, I was down. I felt lost and I found my way. I had low self-esteem, I gave up my power at times. I felt small. I know your pain, I know your confusion, I know the way within, and I know the way out.

Friend, always follow your heart because your heart knows the way. Don't argue with your heart. I know your head may say that your dream or idea is crazy, there's no way you can do this, what will others say or think? I am too old, I don't have money, others already did this ... and so on.

Your heart says yes and that yes has so much power and courage. If you deny that yes to yourself, you will experience suffering. Listen to your heart's calling, make a plan, and get moving. You don't need to figure out the whole plan, all you need to know is what to do next, one step at the time.

The Core Pillars of Grit

There are three pillars that support grit: passion, commitment, and purpose. Remember the Pizza Hut story? My purpose gave me grit. Sometimes you rely on one of those pillars and sometimes you need all three.

Once you find your passion—I am talking now about your life's passion, your life's path or vision—you will want to become the best in what you do. Commit to your art to be the best that you can be. Study every day, learn from the best, apply what you learn. You will become obsessed about getting better doing what you love.

Don't forget it took me a long time to get to where I am today, so if you don't know your passion yet, don't worry. Just remember, get curious and begin exploring. You will find your way, or it will find you.

I remember hearing the word grit a while ago from a very successful friend and client I have, David Moll, an entrepreneur, venture capitalist, and CEO. We were talking about success. These were his words about grit:

We all know that anything worth having isn't easy. And what that translates to mean ultimately, though, is anything worth having takes time. That is why it is not easy. Nothing professionally or personally happens overnight or within a course of a few days, and in time we know we will encounter setbacks, as a simple function of just the way life is. Without the ability to drive through setbacks, we never accomplish any meaningful goals, and hence, that is absolutely the meaning of grit—you can accomplish nothing of importance, nothing of meaning without it.

David is an extremely successful father, husband, athlete, and leader. He carries that grit muscle in everything he does. He said it so well: **anything worth having takes grit.**

When I was young and I dropped things before I finished them, it was because they were not that important to me. That is the simple truth and a hard one to hear sometimes.

I get clients very frequently who come to me because they've tried to lose weight, and they want to figure out why they can't stick with a program. Sometimes, after working with them for a while, we come to a hard moment of truth where I say, "You don't want this bad enough, it is not a priority." If something is important to you, you must give 100 percent commitment to your goal. Ninety-nine percent is not good enough, you must give it your all.

A Priority Issue

I frequently hear, "I don't have discipline, I don't have what it takes, I am not courageous, I am not strong, I don't have time or energy." Those are all just excuses. If you say or think these things, you don't have your priorities right.

In order to achieve success, which is an everyday journey, it takes clarity and planning. A go-with-the-flow philosophy does not work when your vision involves hard work, discipline, and grit. Going with the flow does not work when you need to get things done in a certain way and manner in order to move the needle forward in your success path. If I went with the flow and just wrote when I felt like, this book would not exist. I am not a writer my nature, by gift. I am training myself to be a writer. I have created a weekly schedule where I sit for 90 minutes three times a week and I just write. We can't just do things when we feel like it. We do it even when we don't feel like it. That is commitment and discipline.

Before I started this book, I had the go-with-the-flow philosophy for my writing. You know what it created? Just a vision of a book, a nice wish, a fantasy. That does not get you anywhere, that is just a start, a seed. Then you need to do the work, you need to put in the hours, you need to ask for help when you need it, you need to get educated, you need to show up, you need to do what is hard, you need to practice emotional intelligence during challenges, you need to use your courage and confidence muscles, and you need grit.

What is important to you? Make it a priority. Show that it matters. Make a true commitment with your goal and vision. Get clear, make a priority, and put it on your schedule. Next, manage your energy and give full attention to one task at a time. Do at least one task every day that will move you toward your goal. That strategy builds momentum, your goal will gain strength and life force. You can't just rely on willpower. That life force will help you to find your own state of flow, optimal creativity, and actions with purpose. In this zone, you are extremely efficient and productive. If what you do every day becomes merely a product of willpower, that will take the joy out of it. Willpower used for the long term becomes a passion killer and an energy robber.

I am not saying that sometimes you don't rely on willpower. We all do. We all have those moments when we'd rather drink mimosas instead of going for a run on a Sunday morning. This is when commitment and discipline kick in. You can have the mimosas later!

When you are using your grit muscle, you are focused, you are not doing everything on your list. That is not what grit is used for. Grit fosters tasks that matter, therefore, you will by default inhibit distractions. This is why the combination of grit and discipline help you to organize yourself, your thoughts, your schedule, and your energy. When I sit to write, I don't check my email, Facebook, or text messages. I write until I am done or the time is up. I set my timer for 90 minutes and I write.

High achievers are incredibly focused. They have rituals and daily habits that get them in the mood to create and be in the excellence zone. They are fierce when it comes to protecting their creativity and productivity time. Nothing gets in the way, except emergencies. When you organize your day and your schedule, you actually create more freedom, you create more time to play, and you eliminate the energy of making decisions. Any time you stop to make a decision of what to do next, your energy is being drained. Time is being wasted.

A lot of people have the idea that creating a daily priority list of tasks and scheduling everything creates rigidity. I think it is quite the opposite—it creates freedom, it creates peace of mind just by knowing that you are on track. You are focused, you are clear, and you will handle unexpected challenges as they come because you have the confidence to do so. That is the warrior attitude. And that is you. If you feel you are not there yet, all you need is training. I am giving you a whole training program in this book to become a life success warrior. In the last chapter, I will share how you put it all together to find and develop all these strengths in you. You already have it all. It is just like a muscle—you learn what it takes to make it stronger, do the work, and your body transforms. It's the same with your mind and your habits—they will transform with consistent work and practice.

Don't Worry About How

How many times have you planned a day or a project and things went completely different than you thought? You got stressed and you fought the whole way because you were attached to the process.

Let me save you future headaches and pain. Know the goal, the experience you want to have, the strategies you might use, have the end in mind, and let go of the rest. **Know the start, know the end, and don't stress about the how**. That will flow as you go.

How, you ask? I will mention this book again as an example. The start: I know the theme of my book, I know my goal. The end: I know I want the book ready by June 2017 and prints ready by August 2017. The how: Just sit and write! It flows.

I had no idea what I was going to write exactly. I did a framework of important words, topics, and content for each chapter, drafted it all on paper, and just started writing. Even here, right now, I have no idea what I am going to write in the next paragraph. It just comes to me; this is all about using my creativity and listening to my own intuition. All the knowledge of this book is sitting inside my brain from the years of research, studies, and daily strategy applications. Can you imagine painting a canvas having to know exactly what the next brush stroke had to be? That would be miserable.

What about when you need to have a hard conversation with someone and you rehearse what you're going to say, then you find your talk goes completely different than planned? This happens in my presentations all the time. I used to rehearse a lot before my talks, then I found it was a waste of time. All I needed were my outlines; the rest came in the moment, in the flow. **The zone of flow is where your most creative work will come from.**

So here is the system: Use your left brain (conscious mind) to make the decisions for the year, month, week, or day. Organize, prioritize, and energize. Then let your right brain assist you to get into the flow and show your brilliance.

The Monster Against Grit
Resistance

By now you understand that grit is a must-have muscle to cultivate a successful life, that in times of great challenges you act with your grit. Some life challenges are clear, they come with a big thump, a scream, a loud voice—like you get fired, your boyfriend breaks up with you, you are called by the IRS saying you owe thousands of dollars in taxes, or you get sick.

When you are working on anything that matters to you, you will face challenges along the away.

Here's the deal: the moment you make a decision to pursue your goals with the greatest attitude of grit, determination, discipline, and dedication you will be met with the monster. This monster is a force that shows up to keep you small, to keep you the same, to weaken your confidence, to say that you are not good enough. Call it ego, fear, shadow, your small self, or, simply, the resistance. Whatever you want to name it, you know what it feels like and what it looks like. It is a force that wants to make you stop; a force that wants to make you procrastinate; and a force that wants you to get distracted with emails, Facebook, text messages, and other little things that will eat up your time and energy. The result is poor productivity. A cycle of poor productivity will no doubt suck your confidence and self-esteem. If you are "working hard" and getting nowhere, or don't feel that you are moving forward toward your goal, your passion will dim. If passion dims, grit dims. If you fall into that crevasse of weak passion, it will take a tremendous amount of energy to reignite it. It will take deep grit. You can do it, but why go there? Why fall into that abyss if you can prevent it? Follow my strategies and you will never fall into that abyss because you will be focused, productive, and determined to make it happen.

The bottom line is resistance will try to push you down, but you can stand strong and move through resistance with courage, grace, and power. You don't push resistance because you know if you do, it can get stronger. Have you ever arm wrestled? What happens when you want to win and you apply more force? Your opponent will apply more force too, and the one who can endure the longest will win. Well, life is not arm wrestling. You don't want to fight the monster that can gain strength with your willpower actions, thinking you are David against Goliath. You will win with intelligence and not force. A simple minute of deep belly breathing and a vision of your dream where you feel the results and your success can take that monster down with no force, but with pure power.

This is what Steven Pressfield, one of my favorite writers, shares in his book, *Do the Work:*

Don't prepare. Begin.

Remember, our enemy is not lack of preparation; it is not the difficulty of the project or the state of the market place or the emptiness of the bank account. The enemy is resistance. The enemy is our chattering brain, which, if we give it as much as a nanosecond, will start producing excuses, alibis, transparent self-justifications, and a million reasons why we can't/shouldn't/won't do what we need to do.

Start before you are ready.

Why Do We Resist Change and Growth?

Isn't it ironic that we resist change, that we are afraid of our own success? There are a few reasons why people don't change or transform, or they let their lives pass by and do nothing extraordinary. One reason is fear. We addressed fear in chapter 6. Remember the false and the real fears? Fear of change is all based on false fears.

We also resist change because we are creatures of habit. Habits are hard to change, right? Give up that ice cream every night because you want to lose weight, quit coffee because your adrenal glands are fatigued, don't check emails after 8:00 p.m. because you want to decompress from stress and sleep better, wake up 15 minutes earlier because you want to meditate. All of these changes are easier said than done.

Changing habits is challenging and you need to approach it with intelligence. First, you need to define the reason you want to let go of something—a strong reason that really matters to you. It has to be important. Then you trick the brain because anytime you reach for that coffee or the ice cream, you brain is releasing dopamine, the happy neurotransmitter. It makes you feel good. We need to set our mind to think we are adding something to our life—not taking something away—like more energy or a stronger body. If we focus on what we are losing, like the ice cream pleasure, we tend to not stick with the plan. Thing gain, not lost.

You can't simply remove the pleasure maker, you need to replace it with something that will still feel rewarding to the brain and give you the results you want. The action needs to be aligned with your goals. Ice cream isn't aligned with your goal to lose 15 pounds, but a small apple with almonds is. The dream needs to matter, a lot. Otherwise you will go back to old habits. With a dream that matters, grit develops through the practice of healthy habits.

Okay, now back to the fears of success. The truth is, most people have limited beliefs about success. The limited beliefs that are in your conscious and subconscious levels are directing your attitude and behavior.

Here are some common myths about seeking or having success:

- I am afraid of being too busy.
- I need to have a lot of money to start my own business.
- I don't have the genes to be rich.
- I have to work hard all the time to be successful.
- Money is evil.
- I will have too much stress and lose my health.
- I am not smart enough to be a (fill in the blank).
- I won't make enough money to support my family.

These are all forms of excuses and chatter from the brain, as Pressfield was describing. Being in your head all the time and letting your conscious mind command your life is a death sentence for new ideas, life's vision, and dreams. The brain will always create resistance. Just expect it. I am saving you time and energy by just telling you that. The monster will come, and I am giving you the best weapons to take it down. You can win all the time, but you need to be aware when it is there and take your weapons out with love, courage, and grit.

When the Paralysis Hits

Just get started, move, build momentum. Break the inertia.

I am sharing this because I want to prepare you for the moments of paralysis you will experience. They will happen. It happened to me a lot when I started my business. I would have a break from clients and sometimes I would just stare at my desk, my computer frozen, overwhelmed with how much I thought I had to do to be successful. False fear!

Paralysis will destroy your productivity, and it will therefore weaken your courage and grit. Do everything you can to avoid paralysis. It's inevitable, but I am going to share the key weapon to get away from paralysis. You must develop a habit that every successful person practices daily: a priority projects list. You need to write it down on your "to do" list, your goals for the day, every day. Otherwise, you will get lost, overwhelmed, and freeze. I won't let you do that.

Before we get into details here, you need to first break down your project or business in phases.

When I opened Vitalé Studio in 2015, I wanted to coach clients, develop coaching systems for the workforce in stress and energy management, write a book, do webinars, and create an online course. Plus, run a business by myself. I wanted to do it all.

In a short time, I realized this was insanity. I had the help of a mentor/coach, Dr. James Rouse. He gave me the best advice: do what you love every day, just what you love. The rest will unfold. So, I did that. I coached clients and wrote my book. That is all I focused on. Of course, sometimes we need to do things we don't love, like taxes, cutting budgets, or having a hard conversation with a client. However, those things become very small when we stayed focused on what we love.

Phase one was to build clients. I was very fortunate to build that quickly when I opened. To support my journey, I hired someone to manage my website and do my newsletters, I blocked out three mornings a week to write, and I had time to manage the business needs with no effort. I called this phase two. Phase three, post writing this book, is research for a next book and an online program so I can help more people. Phase four: who knows?

Get clear about what you want, your goals, and break it down into phases. Focus on two to three things max. Keep it simple. Whatever you choose to focus on, do it every day. Do too much and all those false fears will become your reality. Don't ever forget that whatever you choose to do is because you love it. It is because it gives you joy and fulfillment. Start feeling like you are doing too much, too fast, and your joy dies. That is not the purpose, that is not success. You don't want to just create a fat bank account or reach a goal for the sake of it; you want to feel joy in everything you do.

Take these steps to **avoid paralysis and become super productive:**

- Get a small notebook or a notepad and always have it with you.
- Every morning, before work, make a list of the most important things you need to do that day.
- Use an ABC system. Next to each task, put an **A** if that task is a MUST DO, put a **B** if it is a SHOULD BE DONE, and put a **C** if it would be NICE IF DONE TODAY.

These simple strategies will change the way you work and your life. I learned this from Brian Tracy, a self-made millionaire; brilliant author; and expert in sales, success, and time management.

Every time I do these things, I nail my day. I end the day feeling successful, and then I can just play and not worry. This will eliminate that feeling that you should always be working because there is so much to do. We will never get everything done. Make peace with that. Become a master in productivity using these strategies. Being busy is not the same as being productive and effective.

Most people are living with so much unhealthy stress, with the feeling of rush and guilt that they should be working all the time. If you are working all the time and not having any fun, not exercising, skipping meals, drinking coffee all day to stay awake, and not playing with friends and family, you are killing yourself slowly. This is not successful living, it is not sustainable at all, and it is not a way to live your life. This is the recipe for chronic stress, which makes people sick every day. Chronic stress contributes to heart disease, ulcers, stroke, gastrointestinal issues, migraines, and much more. It is also a big contributor to cancer.

Work hard, but with a purpose. Thrive, don't just survive.

Journal Time

- On a scale of 1 to 10, how much grit do you have?
- What area(s) in your life do you wish to have more grit? Why?
- What are your passions in life?
- Are you passionate about your work? If not, why?
- What would it be like to feel passionate about your work every day? (Only answer if you said no to the previous question.)
- When in the past did you have the most grit? What were the drivers?
- What is your plan, from now on, to develop more grit "muscles"?
- Describe your new daily practice for grit.

Final Notes

Putting All the 7 Mind-Sets Together

I am going to start these final notes by sharing what I do daily to develop the seven mind muscles for a fit mind and a fit life.

Awareness

As the most important aspect of changing, creating, and transforming our lives, awareness is the first practice of the day for me.

I develop awareness by sitting in meditation every day for 15 to 20 minutes before work. The word meditation pushes many people away because of the misconception. Meditation does not imply emptying the mind, even though with practice, after a while, you will be able to achieve that.

My Meditation Style

I choose beautiful music for the background—instrumental is best. If you use Pandora, try the meditation station. There are many resources you can choose from.

I choose a place that has sunshine or at least natural lighting. I set the timer on my phone, sit on a yoga block, and close my eyes. I first take three strong belly breaths and exhale slowly. In that moment, I am choosing to become fully present with what is, meaning my body, sensations, feelings, and emotions I am experiencing in the moment.

For the first part of my meditation, I go to gratitude. I think of three to five things that I am very grateful for. These are not just related to work or relationships but also things that no one can take away from me, like the sun, the trees, the sound of the birds, my breath, my courage, and my power.

For the second part, I visualize my goals manifested. What is it like to have that dream realized? I take myself into that place as it is happening right now. I feel what it is like to have financial freedom, to live in the house I want, to travel the world, to share the stage with the top authors and speakers in the transformation arena. The more specific I can be, the better. I spend a few minutes there, really aware of the emotions those scenes bring to me. I am charging my thoughts as I visualize my dreams.

For the third part, I ask for guidance—any message, a word, an object. This is when I really open myself to divine wisdom, when I ask the Force of the Universe to help me. You might call this Source, God, or, simply, Spirit. It does not matter what you call it. Sometimes I call for angels, my grandmother, or my heroes who are no longer with us in this world. Just tap into this creative and intuitive energy that is around you, us, all the time.

And for last part, which is very important to me, I declare my intention for the day. *I am showing up today with strength, courage, and love.* Those words are my core values, I embody them by saying them in silence or out loud. That helps to anchor each word into my subconscious mind and into my day. It really works, it is like making a deep commitment with myself about how my day is going to be, regardless of what happens externally.

This is just my model. Many clients ask me to teach them my model and they really like it. It gives them structure and many people like that, especially beginners. Try it and then let your inner voice guide you. You can also use meditation time to resolve current issues in your life, ask for guidance, search for answers. All of these things are inside you.

STILLNESS IS AN ACTION

Sometimes stillness is one of the most important actions. The art of living comes with knowing when it is time to stay in stillness and when it is time to get out and get busy doing the work. My advice in times of doubt, confusion, stress, or fear is to choose stillness. Stillness gives you space to access your right brain, your intuition, and your divine wisdom. You can't always resolve problems by accessing the same part of you that created the problem—your left brain and your rational mind. Get out of your head and get to the heart where the answers are. Use caution, for sometimes you will not like the answer and that is when courage to listen and to act come in. You've got courage, no doubt. So listen, no matter what.

LISTENING TO THE BODY

Another way to develop high levels of awareness outside meditation is by listening to what your body is telling you.

My mentor, coach, and friend Dr. James Rouse gave me a simple tool to listen to my body. He said, "Alex if your body contracts, run. If it relaxes, it is the place to be." This is not to be taken literally, but basically tells us what to pay attention to. It means your body will be in either a state of contraction and tension when things don't feel right or when your actions are not in alignment with your values and goals, or your body will be in a state of excitement, joy, and relaxation. The more we pay attention to these states and make the changes we need to, the stronger our awareness becomes. This is our inner compass constantly giving us directions. It is one of our true powers. Try it the next time you are around people talking, in a meeting listening, or engaging by yourself with any task. Feel what your body is telling you.

In summary, awareness comes anytime you become present with yourself and your senses. Start being more and doing less. After all, we are human beings, not human doings.

Beliefs

Beliefs get us in trouble many times. It sets our course of thoughts, behaviors, and emotions.

I know I need to reevaluate my beliefs when I am confronted with challenges and conflicts. In those times I choose stillness by sitting in meditation, walking in nature, or journaling. I tap into my wisdom that comes from life experiences or Universal Laws. I also ask the question, "What would love do?" That puts me in a state of accessing my heart, compassion, and empathy, with myself and others involved.

I ask myself where my emotion of fear is coming from. It is usually coming from a deep-seated belief, and that is when I decide if I need to challenge or change my own beliefs, or make a call based on the beliefs and core values that are working for me.

Awareness, compassion, honesty, and love are all prerequisites to transforming our beliefs. This is the arena of growth, transformation, and where the soul evolves. It is the arena where we find freedom.

Confidence

Confidence comes from taking action. We don't wait to have confidence in order to act; we act and confidence gets cultivated.

I work my confidence muscle by challenging myself every week to do something out of my comfort zone, like asking a company if I can come and speak about stress and success. I ask for help, I write a blog, I make video blogs, etc. All these actions make me feel vulnerable, they push me to become more confident.

I also practice confidence by creating daily goals that move me closer toward my life's vision. It may be making a simple phone call, writing an email, or creating a workshop. I take a small step that boosts my confidence in myself.

In summary, find what it is necessary for you to step closer toward your goals. What is the one thing you know you need to do that you have resistance to? Choose that task, and do it. Know what areas you need to develop more confidence in and take an action every day, or at least once a week, that will build that muscle. The more frequent, the better.

Drive

I have three words for drive: movement, motivation, and momentum. They feed our drive and get us to where we want to go. We also must manage our energy to sustain our drive and performance.

When I have my moments of paralysis and I absolutely don't fell inspired to do what needs to be done at the moment, I go for a walk with my dog, or I stretch and do some breathing exercises. I move, I work out, or I meditate. When we freeze, we can get flooded with the emotions under fear, like doubt, insecurity, and inadequacy. We must move and not let those emotions settle in. I deal with them almost weekly, but I don't fuel them. I acknowledge that they are present and I change the focus by choosing movement. The movement can be anything. It may be sitting in meditation, it can be going to the gym, going for a run, calling someone for help—just move the energy. Where energy goes, energy flows. It is all about changing the focus.

The mind can't hold more than one thought at the time, so the key, when fear wants to anchor in us and hold us down, is to change the thought and turn our attention to a different target. Stare at fear too long and it will take control of you. Move and fear will weaken. Tony Robbins says the best antidote to cure fear is gratitude. You can't be in a state of gratitude and fear at the same time. This is so true.

What if the motivation is not there for me? What if I feel flat? That rarely happens now, but when it does, I question what is going on with my emotions, why I am not motivated to be doing what I love. The answers can be boiled down to two things for me: 1. I am mentally tired and need a full day off, or 2. I am spending too much time on tasks that are not very important me, they are draining my energy, and I am distracting myself.

So the solutions are simple. If I am just tired, I take time to rest and restore. I sleep in, I have a massage. In the case of the latter, I reorganize my thoughts and tasks. I reevaluate what my goals for the week/month/year are and get very clear about what needs to happen in order for me to be on track and moving in the right direction. If I can't find the answer, I seek guidance with one of my coaches.

When we choose to move and motivate toward any action that will break the paralysis, we build momentum. Many people get stuck because they keep overanalyzing what the right action is. Any healthy action is better than doing nothing at all. Once we build momentum, insights and inspiration can emerge. A great example is when I do my educational videos for my YouTube channel. Many times I don't know what I will talk about. I set the lights, I get the chalkboard clean, I set the camera, and I start playing with words. Then, voilà! The video is done.

To keep your drive muscle going strong, you must be a solution-oriented type of person and strengthen your positive mind-set. Recognize the challenge and move toward resolution. That will boost your motivation, confidence, and drive. Plus, it will make you grittier—all the super-mind muscles you need for success.

Energy

I energize my body with a great breakfast first thing in the morning. I love almond flour pancakes with yogurt, berries, bananas, and a fresh cup of organic French roast coffee.

After breakfast, I energize my mental source by reading for 45 minutes. I usually read a spiritual or personal growth book. I also love reading psychology and neuroscience books.

Then I walk my dog for 25 to 30 minutes where I start organizing my thoughts for the day, energize my spirit by appreciating the sun, the trees, and the fresh air. I usually get great insights during my walk.

As soon as I get to work I meditate. Then I am ready to rock my day.

You may say that is a lot of time, and it is. I wake up at 5:00 a.m. every morning to fit in all these rituals. They are the source of my daily energy, that is how I charge my batteries. By continuing the mind-set I create in the morning of appreciation, stillness, and peace, I create greatness in my day, every day. I feel energized all day long. I feed my body properly with real wholesome meals at lunch and at dinner. I move, and I connect with people deeply. All these things are energy generators.

At the end of my day, I finish with a great hot bath.

The secrets of creating a great day are to know what your essential needs are. What foods do you need to eat for energy, how do you need to move your body, what mental "food" do you need? How are you connecting with the spirit in you and in the Universe? These are fundamental questions that you need to find the answers to. Before you even know what you want in life, you must know what your body and your biology need in order to function at optimal levels of energy and vitality.

Master your energy, know what drives you every day, and nothing will stop you.

Emotional Fitness

This is where we develop our emotional intelligence, which is our ability to control our emotions in a way that will serve us and others involved.

I work my emotional fitness by checking in with myself daily. I ask, "How do I feel? What emotions am I experiencing now?" I usually do this during my morning walk or meditation. If I am under emotional stress due to a conflict with my partner, for instance, I go to the tenets of conflict, responsibility, and accountability. I inquire what my participation was, how I contributed to the conflict, and how I can contribute to the solution. This requires me to be honest, vulnerable, and courageous.

During emotions of fear, like insecurity and self-doubt, I inquire where the emotions are coming from. Is there an old wound that needs attention and healing? Or is it just a subconscious thought-belief that needs to be transformed? Usually those two questions will present the answer. I take control of my thoughts, behaviors, and actions based on the answers I hear. In my experience and research, this is the most effective exercise to strengthen our emotional intelligence.

The key is always to approach yourself with compassion and love during these inquiries, never judgment or criticism.

Emotional fitness will serve every area in your life because every area, from intimate relationships to business, will present challenges that will trigger your self-worth and self-esteem. As you become emotionally fitter, you become fit for life. That is the way of a warrior.

Fearlessness

A fearless attitude comes from knowing our fear and having the confidence that we can move through it. We arm ourselves with the right weapons to fight fear with grace and precision. The main weapons I use are courage, determination, and focus. There are many others we can rely on, like support from others, knowledge (including self-inquiry and education), and learning more about what we are really dealing with.

My daily practice to cultivate a fearless attitude is to focus on what needs to be done in order to accomplish or take a step forward toward my goal. Once I know what needs to be done, fear sometimes shows up. For instance, fear shows up when I want to contact someone and ask for their help. The fear form is insecurity. Will I say the right words? Will he think this is good enough? Fear shows up before I do my talks in the workforce, when I present to really smart people, when I am vulnerable. Will they judge me? Will they think what I am saying is cool or interesting? I do it anyway, I choose courage. The key here for me is preparation.

My latest method of practice has been to become fully present. I read somewhere that "in the present moment, there is no stress." Most of the time, stress is actually fear. Stress comes with uncertainty and vulnerability. Many times when people say, "I am stressed out," what they are really saying is, "I am scared." But no one wants to admit that.

I deal with fear every single day through the process of expanding my coaching business. Writing this book is scary. I am making myself totally vulnerable. Will readers like it? Will the editor think this sucks? Is my English proper? Fear of judgment sneaks in once in a while. Even though I deal with fear frequently, I choose to not give fear my attention. I see it is there and I keep moving, I keep doing my work, I keep doing what I love, what is my calling. That takes the force away from fear. You can feed it or you can starve it, the choice is yours. Don't freeze, don't paralyze for too long because fear loves paralysis. It is like a virus that can enter much deeper if you are stuck. Move, no matter what it is, move away. I am not saying run away and ignore it. Never ignore fear. Look it in the eye and say, "I got you and I am going to fight you by showing up to myself, showing up to my work, and showing up to my people. Get out of my way." That is my attitude—that is living fearlessly.

Create a practice, find rituals that cultivate courage, like exercise, meditation, or calling someone. Write a mantra for yourself or a quote that really speaks to you and memorize it. Write it down on sticky notes and put them everywhere until you embody the words with every single cell in your body.

You are brave. Do your work and show up.

Grit

Doing what you love, following your call day in and day out, and not giving up. That is grit.

In the movie *Joy*, Jennifer Lawrence played a woman with many struggles, ordinary ones you may say. But she believed in her idea when no one else did. She created a cleaning mop concept and had many failures before her Miracle Mop became a success. That story is all about grit. She cried, she suffered, she fell, but she never, ever gave up.

My dream is not to invent a new product and patent it. Maybe it's not yours either, but we all have a unique product to offer because we are each unique. There is no one in the world like you who has had your experiences, has your perception, or has your mind. Your product, your art is an extension of you. It does not matter if you are an entrepreneur or an employee; what you do is unique and it has the quality of excellence.

I develop the grit muscle by not letting my fear stop me, by not letting people who don't believe in my idea to hold me back. I don't listen to judgment, which ties in with living a fearless life. You don't listen to the voice that wants to keep you small. You don't hang out with the people who want to see you shrinking to match their low level of courage. Don't follow the crowd. You are a leader, so show up as a leader. Inspire others by living at your highest self.

My grit gets weak when I deviate from my passion, when I choose to do something because everyone else is doing it. Anytime I compare myself to others, I risk getting caught up in deep fear and weakening my grit muscle. Passion is the most fundamental fuel for grit, which will spill over into discipline, determination, and resilience.

Keep the light on your passion strong by defining what needs to be done that will create the experiences in life that you want. Sometimes we get too attached to what the specifics are when we need to focus more on what experiences we wish to have. Like, why do I want to create financial freedom? Because I want to experience other cultures, I want to travel, I want to experience giving vacations to my family, and paying for things that they can't afford. I want to experience fine wines and fine food all over the world because I appreciate culinary art. I want to experience living in a house with a big porch where neighbors gather for a glass of wine. I want to experience having a place in the mountains surrounded by nature where I can create daily retreats for clients, where I can cook for them and teach them mindful and holistic living.

We cannot forget the experiences we want, otherwise, our goals can feel dry, flat, and even pointless. We must always find the meaning in our goals and actions, which connects all to the heart. When we only feel driven by the intellect and the ego, we create a life that is not fulfilled. That is not success. Success is having a fulfilled life.

Don't ever give up on your dreams, because your dreams matter. The world wants to see what you create. The time is now; if not now, when?

My Final Note To You

I wrote this book because I want to help and inspire you. I want to be your cheerleader, the one here for you in the times you feel weak or down. I believe in you, I believe in your dreams, and I believe that the only one who can stop you is yourself. I am here to tell you that you must say yes to your dreams, to your happiness because you deserve it. No matter what your past was, what your downfalls are, you deserve to be happy and successful. All you have is now.

From the bottom of my heart, I ask that you love yourself and let go of any judgment of yourself. Embrace all parts of you and forgive yourself! I bet whatever is holding you back can be resolved in a second, the second that it takes for you to just say YES to life. Can you say yes? It is just a decision. One decision has the power to change your whole life.

I became a lifestyle coach because I wish I had had a coach to mentor me when I was young, to tell me: *Alex, you can do anything you want. And these are the books you should read. Here are the qualities you must master. I will be your mentor.*

Nobody showed me a map, nobody told me to follow my dreams, nobody showed me the path to success. I am grateful that I was born with a tremendous sense of curiosity and a spirit of adventure. I was unhappy and I could not accept that. That was a blessing, that was my drive to find my destiny, my path. I am so grateful to that unhappy period of my life. Without those challenges, I would not be writing this book for you and teaching what I believe is very valuable information.

I am here for you. I am your coach, your friend, your mentor. Count on me. Know that I want you to succeed, I want you to be happy, and I want you to experience the most vibrant health. That matters to me deeply.

I need your help because when you are living a life of joy, when your health is vibrant, and you are living your dream life, you will inspire others to follow in your steps to success.

I can't change the world alone, so please join me. Join my army of love, health, and happiness. Let's leave this world better than we found it. You can make so much difference with your talent and unique gifts.

Thank you for being here with me, for reading my book, for trusting me as your coach. I would love to hear from you. You can email me personally at Alex@vitalestudio.com.

With so much love,
Alex

Recommended Reading

EMOTIONAL AND MENTAL FITNESS
You Are the Placebo: Making Your Mind Matter by Dr. Joe Dispenza

Breaking the Habit of Being Yourself: How to Lose Your Mind and Create a New One by Dr. Joe Dispenza

The Power of Your Subconscious Mind by Dr. Joseph Murphy

The Breakthrough Experience: The Revolutionary New Approach to Personal Transformation by Dr. John F. Demartini

Mindset: The New Psychology of Success by Carol S. Dweck, PhD

Power vs. Force: The Hidden Determinants of Human Behavior by David R. Hawkins, MD, PhD

As a Man Thinketh by James Allen

Grit: The Power of Passion and Perseverance by Angela Duckworth

Emotional Intelligence: Why It Can Matter More Than IQ by Daniel Goleman

The Biology of Belief: Unleashing the Power of Consciousness, Matter & Miracles by Bruce H. Lipton, PhD

SPIRITUAL FITNESS
Courage: Overcoming Fear and Igniting Self-Confidence by Debbie Ford

The Places That Scare You: A Guide to Fearlessness in Difficult Times by Pema Chödrön

A Return to Love: Reflections on a Course in Miracles by Marianne Williamson

The Untethered Soul: The Journey Beyond Yourself by Michael A. Singer

The Power of Awareness by Neville Goddard

HAPPINESS TRAINING
The Happiness Advantage: The Seven Principles of Positive Psychology That Fuel Success and Performance at Work by Shawn Achor

The Art of Possibility: Transforming Professional and Personal Life by Rosamund Stone Zander and Benjamin Zander

GOALS-SETTING TRAINING
The ONE Thing: The Surprisingly Simple Truth Behind Extraordinary Results by Gary Keller

Maximum Achievement: Strategies and Skills That Will Unlock Your Hidden Powers to Succeed by Brian Tracy

Start with Why: How Great Leaders Inspire Everyone to Take Action by Simon Sinek

The Big Leap: Conquer Your Hidden Fear and Take Life to the Next Level by Gay Hendricks

ENERGY COACHING
Be Excellent at Anything: The Four Keys to Transforming the Way We Work and Live by Tony Schwartz

Life Unlocked: Seven Revolutionary Lessons to Overcome Fear by Srinivasan S. Pillay, MD

Frequency: The Power of Personal Vibration by Penney Peirce

WELLNESS
How to Eat, Move, and Be Healthy by Paul Chek

Self-Healing with Breathwork: Using the Power of Breath to Increase Energy and Attain Optimal Wellness by Jack Angelo

Think Eat Move Thrive: The Practice for an Awesome Life by Dr. James Rouse and

Dr. Debra Rouse

Recipe

My Favorite Breakfast as mentioned on my daily practice for optimal Energy.

Almond Flour Pancakes
(Makes 3)

½ cup almond flour
2 pasture-raised eggs
½ teaspoon cinnamon
½ teaspoon aluminum-free baking powder
1 teaspoon ground flaxseeds

In a medium bowl, whisk together all ingredients. Coat a skillet with coconut oil or grass-fed butter and heat over medium. Pour a spoonful of batter into the pan for each pancake, and cook each side until firm and a little brown.

For toppings, try grass-fed vanilla yogurt with organic blueberries and bananas, or any fruit of your choice.

I enjoy my pancakes with a fresh cup of organic French roast coffee.

About the Author

Alex Gil lives in Boulder, Colorado, with her partner, Kristen, their sweet dog, Copper, and tiny cat, Sunshine.

She owns Vitalé Studio, a holistic coaching studio, where she helps her clients achieve full levels of health, energy, and success.

When Alex is not working, she is restoring her energy in nature, often mountain biking and running on the trails in Crested Butte.

Contact Alex Gil at Alex@vitalestudio.com.

55827677R10091

Made in the USA
Middletown, DE
18 July 2019